Theatre Royal
—STRATFORD EAST—
'a pioneering theatre' New York Times

†tal

pre

High Heel Parrotfish!

by Christopher Rodriguez

First performed at Theatre Royal Stratford East
Friday 8 April 2005.

Theatre Royal Stratford East
Gerry Raffles Square
Stratford
London
E15 1BN

www.stratfordeast.com

Theatre Royal
STRATFORD EAST
'a pioneering theatre' New York Times

High Heel Parrotfish!
by Christopher Rodriguez

Cast in order of appearance

Lucy Child	**Nicholai La Barrie**
Vashti Kunari	**Raj Ghatak**
Juana La Venezolana	**Anthony Ofoegbu**
Suzy	**Brian Green**
Betty Boo	**Ashley Campbell**
Leandra	**Sandra Bee**
Kitty Caress	**Peter Straker**

Creative Team

Writer	**Christopher Rodriguez**
Director	**Paulette Randall**
Musical Director/Composer	**Felix Cross**
Designer	**Libby Watson**
Choreographer	**Omar F Okai**
Lighting Designer	**James Farncombe**
Sound Designer	**Al Ashford**
Assistant Director	**Robert Hutchinson**
Fight Director	**Nicolas Hall**
Voice Coach	**Julia W Dixon**
Deputy Stage Manager on the book	**Roshni Savjani**
Observers	**Ali Pretty, Michele D'Acosta**

Theatre Royal Stratford East from 8 April to 7 May 2005.

An interview was conducted with the writer, **CHRISTOPHER RODRIGUEZ**, and the musical director, **FELIX CROSS**, for *HIGH HEEL PARROTFISH!* The interview was conducted by **MICHAEL SIVA**, press officer at **THEATRE ROYAL STRATFORD EAST**, at the beginning of rehearsals.

Christopher Rodriguez and Felix Cross

What is this play about?

Christopher Rodriguez: It's about a number of drag queens who try to put on a cabaret in Trinidad when drag cabarets are not fully legal. At least dressing up in drag can be seen as gross indecency. They're trying to create an undercover play against the wishes of society and the law.

Where in Trinidad are you from?

CR: I'm from the North. Trinidad is not that big a country. I'm from the capital, Port of Spain.

Felix Cross: I was born in St James. I came here as a baby, many years ago. I'm not telling you when. My parents are still out there. They live in Santa Cruz.

Why did you write a play about drag queens in Trinidad?

CR: The play was originally done in Trinidad in 1996. It really came out of a group of drag queens asking me to write a play for them, because it was coming up to Carnival, and they wanted to do something for Carnival, something that would make money. That's how a lot of us Trinidadians live – always on the hustle – and they were on the hustle to make some money. They just wanted to string a bunch of songs together to make it into a performance, but I said that they might as well make it something that reflects what they are going to do. What would it be like trying to put on a drag show here in Trinidad, knowing that it would all be undercover anyway? So, it was just coming out of that, and just trying to create something that was a bit more realistic.

What are your feelings about how drag queens are perceived in Trinidad?

CR: I don't want to be unfair to Trinidad, because it's more tolerant than other Caribbean countries, maybe because Trinidad is closer to South America. There is one place in Trinidad where drag queen prostitutes hang out, and everybody knows that. Nobody says anything, and they won't be 'bashed', or anything like that. But at the end of the day, their protection is not enshrined in law, so that even if Trinidad appears slightly more tolerant, it doesn't mean it can't be clawed back at any time or at anybody's discretion. There is nothing enshrined in law to protect people, so there's no redress for any violence or discrimination carried out by an individual or any minority group. It is the way the society functions. Officially, it frowns on things like that. It looks down on it. There's another side of it where behind closed doors they won't say anything, but officially if asked what is there stance on the subject, they will say they stand against drag queens or things that are just too far outside the norm, even if they won't get violent about it. On the other side of the coin, at least there are some places in the Caribbean that are far more intolerant than Trinidad.

FC: Aside from the irony, which is clearly set out in the play, through the juxtaposition between this cabaret and Carnival, where they dance to lively calypso music, you have an island that once a year expresses itself by dressing up in clothes that would make a drag queen seem dull by comparison. Trinidad is a very, very camp nation. The butchest men in Trinidad are camp. It's a camp country. They would hate me for saying so, and I'll never be allowed back into Trinidad, so don't print this bit!

Where did calypso music come from?

FC: There are lots of versions of the origins of calypso. It's like Trinidad itself – it's a callaloo mix-up type of music! You listen to it sometimes and you hear the music of West Africa. You listen to it sometimes and you hear the brass tunes from France and Spain. You listen to it and you hear the music of eastern India, of Bengal. You hear the rhyme patterns and lyric lines that come out of the courts of sixteenth-century France. You hear Spanish love songs. You hear the call and response from West Africa. Calypso music over the years has soaked up all those different styles in many different ways.

Why is calypso music played on metal drums?

FC: Until the 1950s, it was illegal to play drums out in the streets. Calypso had to develop along a different line because it had to be played with non-percussion instruments. That obviously influenced it. In 1945, somebody found all these oil drums, lying around. And then, in the way us West Indians are good at, we took somebody else's rubbish and turned it into something creative. If it wasn't for the oil drums – thank you, America – it wouldn't have taken that direction!

What is the difference between calypso music and soca music?

FC: In the early 1970s, soca music was a way of trying to popularise the notion of calypso. Also, it was saying this has fantastic dance rhythms going on, this great energy. Maybe people don't always want to have a history lesson or a political lesson. Maybe it could be a party experience. Let's make the lyrics much simpler. There are some artistes who have used that and have still managed to say, in tabloid bursts, some interesting things.

How will it work putting calypso and soca music on the stage?

FC: It will work fine. I've done it a number of times. You can take any musical form, and it depends on the story. We've got a great story. I think it will work great. The songs are good. Calypso music has a lot of melody. It has a lot of rhythm to it. But it's surprising that calypso music has not been used a lot more in theatre, given that it's a very melodic form, it's easy on the ear, and it's a form in which the lyrics are supremely important, which is pretty much the definition of songs in musicals. It's not surprising, given the lack of black people in theatre.

Could you tell us a bit about your previous work?

FC: I am primarily a composer, a playwright, and then a director. In my day job, I'm the Artistic Director of NITRO. I work a lot writing music for theatre. I've done the music for more than 70 shows, but I've also written plays like *Glory!, Mass Carib,* and *Passports To The Promised Land.* Last year I wrote and co-directed *Slamdunk* with Benji Reid.

CR: I wrote *Clear Water,* which was staged at the Barbican Pit in 2000, and before that there was *Independence Day,* which was at the Oval House. Then, there was a play we did called *Equiano,* about the slave who made a name for himself when he achieved freedom. That was at Everyman in Liverpool, Green Rooms in Manchester – it did a tour, and then came to Oval House in London. That one I really liked, because I was writing in eighteenth-century English. Then I did some Anancy plays for Talawa that came up at Queen Elizabeth Hall and Bloomsbury. I also did a radio play for Radio Three, and it won a Sony gold award, which is the equivalent of an Academy. And, of course, I've also done work in Trinidad.

What plans do you have for the future?

CR: To buy an island off Rio! I have some plays that I need to finish writing, and another play that will hopefully be coming on stage before the end of this year. I just want to look at what I really want to do in terms of being a writer.

FC: As soon as *High Heel Parrotfish!* opens, NITRO goes into residency at the Hammersmith & West London College, where we're devising a show there. I'm directing that. Then, I go to help with the early stages of devising a show called *Twilight* in Manchester with Contact in July. Then, I'm co-producing the European Urban Theatre Festival in Manchester, and then co-producing the second 'NITRO at the Opera' Festival in the New Year, and I'm writing and directing NITRO's next main stage show which has the current working title of *The Wedding Dance.* It's a salsa musical – not the one that closed in the West End after eight days! Also, I'm writing a musical-comedy for the New Wolsey in Ipswich, called *The Man who Pretended to be Married.*

How do you feel this play reflects Stratford East's commitment to develop new talent and new voices?

FC: I'm a really old voice! However, I think you can look at new voices in different ways. They can be the voices of actors, writers and artistes who have never done it before. Then, there can be the voices of artistes who have been ignored, but who have done a bit of work. Then, there are the voices of artistes who have never worked here before, but have worked in lots of other places. This is the first time I've worked fully at Stratford East after over 20 years in the theatre.

CR: Maybe the idea might be a bit new, and maybe the voices of these characters haven't been heard on a British stage before. And that might be important. If it causes some people in the community to think – black homophobia is a hot issue. This play allows these voices to speak out.

Cast in order of appearance

Nicholai La Barrie Lucy Child

Nicholai is originally from Trinidad and started his acting career at the age of ten, with the Lilliput Children's Theatre. He performed with all the major theatre companies in Trinidad and Tobago. He directed *It Had To Be You* for Ragoo Productions and *Pieces of Mine* for Little Caribbean Theatre. Since moving to London, he has appeared in *Clear Water* at the Barbican (as part of BITE 2000), *The Adventures of Snow Black and Rose Red* at Stratford Circus, *Macbeth* at the Oval House and *One Four Seven* for Dende Collective. Nicholai has also taken part in various readings and workshops, including *Passport to the Promised Land* at the Greenwich Theatre and *The Seer* at the West Yorkshire Playhouse. Nicholai is currently Head of Youth Arts and Resident Drama Tutor at the Oval Theatre.

Raj Ghatak Vashti Kunari

Raj received a BA (Hons) in English and Drama from Central School of Speech and Drama at Queen Mary University. Theatre credits include: creating the role of Sweetie in *Bombay Dreams* at the Apollo Victoria (West End). Previously he created the role of Raj in *Hijra* (Bush Theatre and West Yorkshire Playhouse). Other credits include: *My Dad's Corner Shop* (Birmingham Rep); *Airport 2000* (Greenwich Theatre); *West Side Story* (West-End); *Bollywood or Bust* (Watermans Arts Centre); *Don't Look At My Sister Innit!* and *Arrange That Marriage* (Bloomsbury Theatre and National Tour); *East Is East* (Oldham Coliseum) and *Nagwanti* (Tara Arts). Television credits include: *All About Me, Hard Cash, In No Time* and *Out of Sight*. Film credits include: *Never Say Never Mind*, *Birthday Girl* and *Sari and Trainers*.

Anthony Ofoegbu Juana La Venezolana

Film credits: Nicholas Roeg's *Samson and Delilah*; Ian David Diaz' *The Killing Zone* and *Dead Room*, Nigel Barker's *Plato's Breaking Point* and *Heritage* by Ladi Ladebo. Television credits include: Detective Inspector Parrish in *Casualty*, Mr Akinwanda in *Chambers;* Abraham James, in *The Bill* and Ray the Masonic high master in *2 Point 4 Children*. Corporate TV credits include: BBC NEWS 24, BSkyB Sports, Discovery Channel, Ford Cars and

Heinz Soup. Anthony was a member of the BBC Radio Repertory Drama Company from 1997 to 1998; he continues to work for BBC Radio. He has also worked with IRDP (Independent Radio Drama Productions) and other independent radio companies. Theatre credits include: Lincoln in *Topdog/Underdog* for Tall Tales Theatre at the Dublin Fringe Festival (2004). He led the physical cast of Barabbas Theatre Company's *Hurl* as Musa Daboh for both Galway and Dublin Festivals in Ireland (2003); Tutor in Wole Soyinka's play, *King Baabu* (touring South Africa, Lesotho, Nigeria, Switzerland and Germany); Sanda in Soyinka's *The Beatification of Area Boy* (premiered at the West Yorkshire Playhouse and toured Europe, America and Australia). In June 2002 he was in Las Vegas with the Nevada State Conservatory Theatre as Minister in *Oedipus at Colonus* (XI International Festival of Ancient Greek Drama in Delphi, Greece); Devon in *Long Time No See* for Talawa Theatre (Stratford Circus) and an especially written monologue *The Blond* (The Space and The Cockpit Theatre). Physical Skills credits: Ondine King in *Ondine for Melange Theatre* (Cochrane Theatre); Mr Mugglewump in *The Twits* (Belgrade, Coventry). He has 'jitter-bugged' for Zoots and Spangles Dance Theatre supporting Humphrey Lyttleton's musical jazz performances. For Four's Company Dance Theatre his work included *Vice and Joy* and *On the Good Foot* (Theatre Royal Stratford East). Singing credits: Remus in Scott Joplin's ragtime opera *Treemonisha* (BAC and Hackney Empire); Ton-ton in *Once on This Island* (Royalty/Island Theatre, West End).

Brian Green Suzy

Training: The Academy of Live and Recorded Arts, London. Operatic productions include: Opéra National de Lyon (France): *Les Negres*; De Nederlandse Opera (Amsterdam): Les Troyens; Opera North (Leeds): *The Magic Flute*; National Opera of Wellington (New Zealand): *Die Zauberflöte*; Pegasus Opera at the Linbury Studio, The Royal Opera House, Covent Garden: *Carmen*; Grand Opera House (Belfast): *Porgy and Bess*; Opera Australia: *La Bohème*. Others in Australia: *Ruddigore*, *Turandot*, *L'enfant et les Sortilèges*, *Les Mamelles de Tiresias*, *Pagliacci*, *Tales of Hoffman*, *Iphigénie en Tauride*, *The Marriage of Figaro*, *Wide Sargasso Sea*. Oratorio: *St. John Passion*. Musical productions include: Queen's Hall (Trinidad) and West Yorkshire Playhouse (Leeds): *Carnival Messiah*; Royal Botanic Gardens, Sydney: *The Caribbean Tempest*; Brisbane Festival: *Kiss Me Kate*; Melbourne Concert Hall: *Carmen Jones*; Sydney Theatre Company: *Merrily We Roll Along*. Theatre productions include: Brooklyn Academy Of Music (New York), Sydney Theatre Company and Sydney Olympic Arts Festival: *The White Devil*; The Stables Theatre (Sydney): *Been So Long*; Sydney Theatre Company: *Much Ado About Nothing*; Trinidad: Hatuey, *Queen*

of *The Bands*, *The Rocky Horror Show*, *Sons and Mothers*. Television credits include: *West Wood Park*, *Frankie's House*, *Hatuey*. Opera Film: Opera Spanga (Holland), *Rigoletto*. Recently Brian played the role of Joebell in the feature film *Joebell and America*, based on the Earl Lovelace's short story, produced by Caribbean Communication Network. Next is Derek Walcott's *Steel*, directed by Derek Walcott.

Ashley Campbell Betty Boo

Ashley began his training at the Sylvia Young Theatre School. Whilst at Sylvia Young's appeared in *Carmen Jones* at the Old Vic and *Carousel* at the Royal National Theatre. Ashley represented the UK on the *Bad Tour* with Michael Jackson and performed at the *Danny Kay International Awards* with Audrey Hepburn and Roger Moore in Amsterdam in 1991. At sixteen he was accepted on a scholarship to the Arts Educational School in London on their three-year musical theatre course where he graduated in 1999, the recipient of the Ned Sherrin Award for most outstanding all-round performer. Theatre credits include: *Little Shop Of Horrors* (Edinburgh), *Fame* (West End and Tour), Wilson in Joe Ortons's *The Ruffian on the Stair* (Barons Court), Narrator in *No Picnic* (Barons Court), Jed in *Something about Him* (Riverside Studios), Dromio of Syracuse in the critically acclaimed *The Bomb-itty of Errors* (West End), *Big Boys* (Soho Theatre), Moses/Frankie in *Gutted* (Tristan Bates). TV includes *Holby City*, *Bard 2 Verse*, *The Gorgon's Head*, *Let's Write a Story*, *Hevie Revie*, *Misty* (all for the BBC); *London's Burning* (LWT), *The Sex Starved Years*...(Channel 5), *William and Mary* (Granada) and *There's Something About Him* (Independent). Film credits: *Jam*, directed by Angelo Abela.

Sandra Bee Leandra

Sandra has already attracted huge attention and a wide fan base for her portrayal of Petronella, the dancehall queen in the first series of BBC2's hit drama series *Brothers and Sisters*. Amongst several other TV appearances, she performed a camera monologue for the BBC series *Still Here*. On a lighter note, Sandra displayed a whole range of comic characters, ranging from sophisticated to streetwise, when she starred in the fast moving sketch show *Waiting to Inhale* which ran for two sell-out seasons at The Theatre Royal Stratford East before going on a highly successful tour. Sandra demonstrated both her commitment to supporting community theatre and her rapport with young audiences when performing as Princess/Sorceress in the New Peckham Variety Theatre's *Snow Queen*. Last year Sandra took her sell-out one-woman show *A Night to Remember* to Minorca in Spain (first performed at Oval House in 2003). She also acted along side Jack Dee playing his hard nut sidekick Wendy in ITV's comedy drama *Tunnel of Love*. With her gift for physical comedy, drawing on a background as trained dancer, Sandra has built a sizeable following on the comedy circuit in addition to her TV popularity. Sandra can soon be seen in the Miramax film *Derailed* alongside Golden Globe and Bafta Winner Clive Owen.

Peter Straker Kitty Caress

Born in Jamaica, Straker is known to more than one generation of music fans and theatregoers as a unique and versatile performer. He first attracted attention in 1968 when he starred as Hud in the original London production of the seminal musical *Hair*. He has since then appeared on a regular basis in both musical and theatre productions in the West End including: Pete Townsend's *Tommy* (Queens Theatre), *Blues in the Night* (Piccadilly Theatre), Ken Hill's *The Phantom of the Opera* (originally performed at Theatre Royal then at *Shaftesbury Avenue*), *Hot Stuff* (Cambridge Theatre). His classical roles include *Cassius* in *Julius Caesar* at Bristol Old Vic and Lucio in *Measure for Measure* at the National Theatre. In 1997 he appeared in the first London revival of Stephen Sondheim's *Assassins* at the New End Theatre. He appeared in a piece specially written for him, *Mary and The Shaman*, produced by Babel Theatre, which premiered at BAC in December 1998. Peter has also made several appearances on film and television. He starred in Ned Sherrin's ground breaking *Girl/Boy*. On television he has appeared in such diverse roles as *Dev* in Ron Hutchinson's hugely successful series *Connie* with Stephanie Beacham and Pam Ferris; the title role of *Da Silva* in Colin Nutley's *Da Silva Da Silva*; Dr Who's *Destiny of the Daleks* with Tom Baker; *The Orchid House* directed by Horace Ové. Peter's recording career has been no less notable, including collaborations with The Alan Parson's Project and Freddie Mercury's memorable *Barcelona* with Montserrat Caballe. He has also recorded five solo albums, two of which were produced by Freddie Mercury. He appeared in Talawa's *One Love* at Bristol Old Vic and the Lyric Hammersmith, and toured in Kwame-Kwei Armah's *Hold On*, both with Ruby Turner. In 2002 he was in *Sammy* and in 2003 in *Red Riding Hood* as The Wolf, both at Theatre Royal. Last year Peter performed *Straker sings Brel* written and directed by Mel Smith; he also toured *Phantom* in Japan. He is currently working on several new solo projects for the theatre with various collaborators including composer Warren Wills and writer David Evans, as well as a new recording project.

Creative Team

Christopher Rodriguez Writer

Christopher Rodriguez was born in Port of Spain, Trinidad. Before moving to London he worked as assistant director and producer on his plays performed in Port of Spain. Since moving to London he has worked as assistant script editor at BBC Radio Drama, as writer in residence at the Oval House Theatre and was recently given an attachment to the Royal National Theatre Studio. As Talawa's current literary associate, Christopher is responsible for commissioning and developing scripts and chairing Talawa's Channel 4 sponsored Black Writers Skills Group. He is also writer in residence at Lichfield Garrick. UK writing credits include: *Equiano, Independence Day* (Oval House), *Clear Water* (Barbican Pit), *Anansi Steals the Wind* (Queen Elisabeth Hall, Southbank and UCL Bloomsbury) and *A Parandero is Missing* (Radio 3).

Paulette Randall Director

Paulette is Artistic Director for Talawa Theatre Company. Her distinguished career to date has been a mixture of theatre directing, television producing and writing. For Talawa, she has directed *Urban Afro Saxons* (Theatre Royal Stratford East); *Blest Be The Tie* (Royal Court); *Abena's Stupidest Mistake* (The Drill Hall) and the critically acclaimed *Blues For Mr. Charlie* (New Wolsey Theatre, Ipswich, The Tricycle). Other credits include: *King Hedley II* (Tricycle/Birmingham Rep); *Funny Black Women on the Edge* and *Shoot to Win* (Theatre Royal Stratford East); *Two Trains Running* and *Up Against the Wall* (Tricycle); *The Amen Corner* (Bristol Old Vic); *Desmonds* (Channel 4); *Porkpie* (Channel 4); two series of *Comin' Atcha* (ITV); *Blouse and Skirt* (BBC) and *Kerching!* (BBC). Paulette was also producer of the second series of BBC1 comedy *The Crouches*.

Felix Cross Musical Director/Composer

Felix Cross is a composer, playwright, lyricist and director and has been the artistic director of Nitro (formerly Black Theatre Co-op) since 1996. Credits include: *Slamdunk,* (book and co-director); *Passports to the Promised Land* (book, music and lyrics); *Up Against The Wall* (co-writer of book with Paulette Randall) and *Iced* (director). For Nitro, Felix has produced four years of the annual Nitrobeat festival, *A Nitro At The Opera* and, most recently, *Revival!* with the Royal Opera House.

Libby Watson Designer

Libby trained at Bristol Old Vic Theatre School and in theatre design at Wimbledon School of Art. Design credits include: *The Man of Mode* (Northcott Theatre Exeter): *Secret Garden, Beautiful Thing, The*

Changeling, The Tenant of Wildfell Hall, Arabian Nights and *Side by Side by Sondheim* (for Salisbury Playhouse as resident designer); *Othello, Sisterly Feelings, Morning After the Miracle, Twelve Angry Men* and *The Play Called Corpus Christi* (Guildhall); *Airport 2000* (Leicester Haymarket, Greenwich Theatre and Riverside Studios); *The Birds* (Birmingham Rep); *Under Their Influence* (Tricycle Theatre); *The Front Room* (Oval House); *The Wills's Girls* at the Tobacco Factory in Bristol and *Vengeance* (Hackney Empire, Bullion Rooms). Watermill Theatre productions include *Witch, Lone Flyer, Children of the Light, Gigolo, Call to the Sky, Accelerate, I Dreamt I Dwelt in Marble Halls, The Fourth Fold* and *The Comedian*. Libby was Associate Designer for the off-Broadway production of *Humble Boy* at Manhattan Theatre Club, NY, in the West End and for the UK tour. Other UK tours include *Voyagers* and *The Three Servants*. Opera credits include: *Mignon, Beatrice and Benedict* and *Comedy on the Bridget* at GSMD. Productions at Theatre Royal Stratford East include: *Ready or Not, Night of the Dons, An Audience with Angie Le Mar, Cinderella, Funny Black Women on the Edge, Sus* and *Jamaica House*. Other Talawa productions include *Urban Afro Saxons* (Theatre Royal Stratford East); *Blest Be the Tie* (Royal Court Theatre); *The Key Game* (Riverside Studios) and *Blues for Mr Charlie* (Tricycle and Wolsey).

Omar F Okai Choreographer

Omar is the Artistic Director of The Okai Collier Company. His directing credits include: *How To Succeed In Business Without Really Trying* (Rudolph Steiner); *Purlie* (nominated for four What's On Stage Theatregoers Choice Awards 2005); *Ruthless!* (Winner of five Musical Stages awards 2002, including Best Director); *Honk!* (Rudolph Steiner); *A...My Name Is Alice; Elegies; Spooky Noises; Countess and Cabbages; A Time To Speak; Doing Something Right; Viva O Carnaval; Everyone's Opera; La Vie En Rose; Love Loss Life and Laughter; Child of the Jago* (Purcell Room); *Carmen* (Movement, Lindbury ROH); *Five Guys Named Moe* (William Ellis School); *Burleigh Grimes* (Movement Director); *Cabaret* (Frankfurt) and for the RNT assistant choreographer for the Olivier Award-winning *Honk!*; *The Villains' Opera* and *Candide*. Producing credits include: *The Crusaid Requiem* and *Passion*. West End performing credits: *Five Guys Named Moe* (original cast), *Sweet Charity, King* and *My One And Only*. Other credits: *Golden Boy, Elegies, Ain't Misbehavin'* and *Tourette's Diva*. Omar is the Director of *Urban Theatre* and has also worked with Royal Opera House Education, The Roundhouse, Millennium Dance, Arts Educational and The Urdang Academy. For further information visit: www.okaicollier.co.uk

James Farncombe Lighting Designer

Theatre credits include: *Street Trilogy – Car, Raw* and *Kid* (Theatre Absolute, national tour); *Playboy of the West Indies* (Tricycle and Nottingham Playhouse); *Blues for Mr Charlie* (Tricycle and Ipswich Wolsey); *The Fortune Club* (Tricycle and Leicester Haymarket); *Blest Be The Tie* (Jerwood Theatre Upstairs at The Royal Court); *Forward* The Door (Birmingham Rep); *The Maths Tutor* (Hampstead Theatre, London and Birmingham Rep); *Urban Afro Saxons* and *Funny Black Women on the Edge* (Theatre Royal Stratford East); *This Lime Tree Bower* (The Belgrade, Coventry); *To Kill A Mockingbird*, *Master Harold and the Boys*, *West Side Story*, *Death of a Salesman*, *Peter Pan*, *The Witches*, *Plague of Innocence* and *Unsuitable Girls* (all at Leicester Haymarket Theatre); *The Hypochondriac* (nominated Manchester Evening News Awards Best Design Team 2003) and *Popcorn* (Bolton Octagon); *Making Waves*, *Micro Musicals* and *Soap* Steven (Joseph Theatre, Scarborough); *Amy's View* (Salisbury Playhouse and Royal Theatre, Northampton); *Krapp's Last Tape*, *A Different Way Home*, *A Visit From Miss Prothero* (Lakeside Arts Centre, Nottingham); *Beautiful Thing* (Nottingham Playhouse and national tour); *Dead Funny* (York Theatre Royal and Bolton Octagon); *Lord of the Flies, Bloodtide, Road, Rumblefish* for Pilot Theatre Company (York Theatre Royal and national tours); *The Blue Room* and *The Elephant Man* (Worcester Swan Theatre); *Unsuitable Girls* (Sheffield Crucible Studio and tour); *East is East* and *A Women of No Importance* (New Vic Theatre Stoke); *Goldilocks* (Lyric Theatre, Hammersmith); *Mignon* (Guildhall).

James was assistant lighting designer on *The Women in White* and *La Cava* in the West End. Projects for Spring 2005: *Osama the Hero* and *A Single Act* (Hampstead); *Abigail's Party* (York Theatre Royal) and *A Who's Who of Flapland* (Nottingham Lakeside Theatre).

Al Ashford Sound Designer

Theatre credits include: *Blues for Mr Charlie* (Talawa, New Wolsey, Tricycle); *Abena's Stupidest Mistake* (Talawa); *Little Sweet Thing* (Eclipse, New Wolsey, Birmingham Rep and Nottingham Playhouse); *Aladdin, Blithe Spirit, Cinderella, Double Indemnity, Foreign Lands, How the Other Half Loves, Road, Mad World My Masters, Pal Joey, Perfect Day, Robin Hood* and *The Babes in the Wood*, *The Diary of Anne Frank* and *The Turn of The Screw* (Wolsey Theatre and New Wolsey Theatre); *Road, Happy Days, Ion, The Triumph of Love, To Kill a Mockingbird, Twelfth Night, Krapp's Last Tape* (Mercury Theatre, Colchester); 1996 production of *Double Indemnity* (Clwyd Theatr Cymru); *Cinderella* (Hackney Empire); *Mack And Mabel* (The Ipswich Regent); *David Copperfield, The Wuffings, The Timelords of Tacket Street, Tithe War!, Parson Combs and The Ballad of Mad Dog Creek* and *Boudicca's Babes* (Eastern Angles).

Robert Hutchinson Assistant Director

Theatre credits as a writer include: *The Miserable Mansion* (The Hampstead Theatre, 2005); *Ribbons* (BBC Radio London, 2004); *Smile* (The Hampstead Theatre, 2004); *The Carnival King* (The Royal Court Theatre Upstairs 2001).

Theatre credits as a director: *A New You* by Lewis Davies (Soho Theatre, 2005); *Blasted* by Sarah Kane (The Contact Theatre, Manchester, 2004); *Breathe* (The Oval House, 2002). Credits as a writer/director include: *Get it together* (music video artist Anthony Oseyemi) 2004; *A Can Of Madness*, adapted book by Jason Pegler (The Catford Broadway, 2004). Credits as Studio assistant/Runner: MTV – *Outlaws Dennis Hopper* (The Hospital Studios, Covent Garden, 2004); *Guinness Book of Records* – clip show (The Hospital Studios, 2004 for Sky One). Robert also worked as a co-director for The National Youth Theatre at The Nottingham Playhouse in 2003. On the same year he was Assistant Director in *Moon On A Rainbow Shawl*, directed by Paulette Randall (The Nottingham Playhouse, The Bristol Old Vic, The Ipswich Wolsey).

Season Update

September saw the appointment of the theatre's new Artistic Director Kerry Michael. His inaugural production *THE BATTLE OF GREEN LANES* confirmed the theatre's continued commitment to discovering new talent and presenting work by artists not historically represented in British Theatre. First time playwright Cosh Omar told a story of a young Turkish Cypriot man trying to grow up in North London. With interest in New York, Athens and Sydney, plans are afoot for a remount in 2006 with a national and international tour.

"Kerry Michael amply demonstrates that he has his finger on the pulse of London's streets and stages a fabulously acted, brazenly didactic drama." Patrick Marmion, *Daily Mail*, 22 October 2004

"The whole thing carries the unmistakable whiff of authenticity and makes for a fantastic statement of intent about the kind of voices the Theatre Royal wants to hear from over the coming years." Dominic Cavendish, *Daily Telegraph*, 23 October 2004

"Dramatically robust, cleverly staged by the Theatre Royal's new Artistic Director, Kerry Michael, and acted with passion, this is a play for today that raises issues about identity, belonging, brainwashing and tolerance without taking sides." Roger Foss, *What's On In London*, 27 October 2004

The annual Christmas Show came next. **SLEEPING BEAUTY** was written by Hope Messiah and Delroy Murray; two graduates from the theatre's Musical Theatre Workshop. Once again audiences and critics recognised the theatre's commitment to good storytelling, original music and proper investment in this important genre. It was directed by the theatre's Associate Director Dawn Reid.

"Probably the most wholesome panto offering in town; just as likely one of the best." Jonathan Gibbs, *Time Out*, 15 December 2004

"This production proves once again that at Stratford East pantomime is one of the abiding joys of the season." Michael Darvell, *What's On In London*, 15 December 2004

THE BIG LIFE returned and quickly became our most successful show at the box office to date. The critics once again raved about it and the show is a wonderful achievement to all who worked on it, including the show's author Paul Sirett, who first came up with the lovely simple idea to take Shakespeare's *Love's Labours Lost* and set it in the time of the Windrush period; Paul Joseph, who four years ago had never seen a musical and was nurtured through our Theatre Royal Musical Workshops; and Clint Dyer, who did a splendid job not only in directing the show but shaping the work from the outset to produce something genuine, new and vibrant.

"Funny, sexy, touching and tuneful, as well as being blessed with the most tremendous heart, it is a production that must surely find a home in the West End." Charles Spencer, *Daily Telegraph*, 25 February 2005

THE BIG LIFE has now been picked up by commercial producers. It transfers into the West End and starts previewing at the Apollo Theatre, Shaftesbury Avenue on May 11th.

And finally, May 8th has been set as the transmission date for *'Rappin' at the Royal'*, the documentary filmed here last autumn by Blast Films for Channel 4. *'Rappin' at the Royal'* follows eight writers grappling with the process of writing a new musical. The programme also goes backstage at Theatre Royal and includes excerpts of the three shows mentioned above as well as the important work of our education and artistic development departments.

YOUNG PLAYWRIGHTS

Do you want to write a play?
TRSE is looking for young people to join **Young Voices**,
our playwriting programme

If you are aged 16–22 years, live in East London
and are interested in theatre and have a play in your head,
then call us to register.

You will get professional support from Theatre Royal Stratford East to develop your play and you can be part of a new play-reading event.
No previous experience necessary!

The group meets on Monday evenings 6pm – 8pm.
Call Jan on 020 8279 1107 for details of how to join.

For all youth and education activities please call Jan on 020 8279 1107

NEW WORK • NEW VOICES

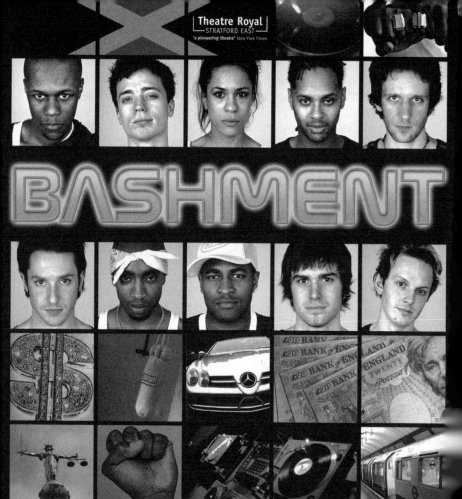

Theatre Royal
— STRATFORD EAST —
'a pioneering theatre' New York Times

BASHMENT

A new play by
Ricki Beadle Blair
From 20th May 2005

BASHMENT

A new play by

Ricki Beadle Blair

Bashment is a new play about love and loyalty, violence and victimization. It is hard-hitting yet tender, serious yet funny.

Bashment is a tale about 10 young people, belonging and being outsiders in London in 2005.

Box Office: 020 8534 0310 | Minicom: 020 8279 1114
Book online: stratfordeast.com (no booking fee)

NEW WORK·NEW VOICES

♟ talawa

About The Company

Talawa Theatre Company is one of the UK's leading voices for Black Theatre. Formed in 1985 and currently led by Artistic Director Paulette Randall, Talawa has continually sought to provide high quality productions that reflect the significant creative role of Black theatre in Britain. Productions include interpretations of universal classics, contemporary Black British plays and commissioned new work. Talawa also provide opportunities for young people with their extensive education and outreach programmes, such as the annual young people's theatre programme and script development services aimed at nurturing a new generation of Black artists.

The Staff

Artistic Director	**Paulette Randall**
General Manager	**Kate Sarley**
Education Associate	**Raidene Carter**
Marketing & Publicity	**Alison Copeland**
Literary Associate	**Christopher Rodriguez**
Finance	**Zewditu Bekele**
Administration	**Philippa Taylor**

Board Members

The Baroness Howells of St Davids (Chair), Pax Allotey, June Baden-Semper, Margo Boye-Anawomah, Jennifer Francis, Joy Nichols, Rudi Page, Dr Marie Stewart, Ben Thomas, Don Warrington, Claudia Webbe

Talawa Theatre Company Ltd
3rd Floor, 23–25 Great Sutton Street
London
EC1V 0DN
Tel: 020 7251 6644
Fax: 020 7251 5969
www.talawa.com

Building A Home For Black Theatre

The first Black owned and managed UK building for promoting and developing the work of Black artists is on its way. Continuing the work of Yvonne Brewster Talawa's founder producer, 2006 will see Central London as home to the first permanent Black theatre with Talawa as its resident company producing their own work and hosting the best productions by other Black companies and artists.

It will be the national and international focus for the training and development of Black writers, performers, creative artists and other theatre workers raising the profile of the work of Black artists and increasing theatre audiences from the Black community. Talawa aims to be the principle promoter, developer and discoverer of seminal new Black British Plays as well as fielding key work in Europe, the Americas and the Caribbean.

Using Black culture and experience to further enrich British theatre, the new complex will provide the arena for high quality productions that reflect the significant creative role of Black theatre and extend the range of culturally diverse work available to audiences.

The new venue is a well-equipped, easily accessible development offering a 300-seat auditorium, a rehearsal space and a Black Theatre Archive and information unit. It will also facilitate education, outreach and community work initiatives contributing to Talawa's overall vision of the space as a centre for the development of Black theatre and a cultural resource for the Black community.

If you or your company would like to join with us and our major funders in partnership to bring about this exciting initiative we would be delighted to show you our business plan and explain the advantages of sponsorship, naming opportunities and the extraordinary public relations benefits of this unique project.

Talawa is a not-for-profit organisation and registered charity governed by a board of trustees. The building project is supported by Arts Council England. Talawa also receives financial assistance from the Millennium Commission and The London Development Agency.

Channel 4 Sponsors Talawa's Black Writers Skills Group!

Channel 4 continues its commitment to support ethnic minorities in the television industry by sponsoring Talawa's Black Writers Skills Group. The programme, which hosts eight to ten Black and Asian writers who have recently had plays produced, concentrates on developing their written, technical and business skills for theatre, television and radio over a period of one year. The programme includes sessions with Graham Whybrow, literary manager of the **Royal Court** and Jack Bradley, literary manager of **The National Theatre**. The programme will climax with each writer creating and directing a 20-minute piece for a showcase at Soho Theatre and Writers Centre in October 2005 as part of their Black History Month Programme. For more information about Talawa's Black Writers Skills Group, or any of our other services please visit www.talawa.com.

The writers group is also sponsored by BBC, Peggy Ramsay Foundation and LWT.

Thursday 18 – Saturday 20 August
Talawa Theatre Company and the Drill Hall present

TYPT:05
Directed and designed by Mem Morrison

Talawa Young People's Theatre is a phenomenon in youth arts: culturally specific and refreshingly progressive, it continues to shatter expectations of 'theatre made by young people' with visually stunning and emotionally engaging productions.

TYPT:05 members will create for five intensive weeks; the result – an unparalleled piece of performance charged with the ideas, energies and emotions of a critical generation.

As yet, there's no name.
As always, there's no knowing.

Booking & show Info: 020 7307 5060
www.drillhall.co.uk

Into challenging theatre?
If you're aged 16-23, Black or Asian* and able to commit for five weeks this summer, please contact Raidene Carter on 020 7251 6644 or email **raidene@talawa.com**.

* Includes African, Caribbean, Asian, East Asian and Middle Eastern heritages. Applications from young people outside these groups will be considered on the basis that they express an attachment to Talawa's mission as a Black organisation (see www.talawa.com).

NITRO, formerly known as Black Theatre Co-operative, is Europe's longest established black theatre companies. Since the establishment of the company in 1978, we have been committed to: *encouraging, commissioning, devising and producing new writing by black British writers. We aim to produce and tour dynamic, innovative and high quality work that expresses the aspirations, cultures and issues that concern black people today*.

Since 1998 **NITRO** has focused that commitment towards Musical Theatre: from hip hop dance musicals to contemporary operas; from traditional musicals to festivals of new work. As well as nurturing emerging black artists we also encourage established and highly successful black artists who work away from theatre in say, music, poetry, film or dance, to come and join us in expanding the boundaries of musical theatre, making it more exciting, more relevant.

SLAMDUNK

UP THE WALL

2004 saw **NITRO** produce its ground breaking national tour of the Hip-Hop musical, *SLAMDUNK* (possibly the longest tour of a hip-hop basketball rap musical in theatrical history), but that wasn't all we did. With Contact in Manchester we developed *RnB*, a course for songwriters interested in writing musicals. Also with Contact and Tara Arts in association with Zion Arts, we ran the third of our hugely successful and influential *Live and Direct* courses for Black and Asian Directors.

A NITRO AT THE OPERA and **REVIVAL!**

2005 looks like being equally busy and exciting. Straight after *High Heel Parrotfish!* we will be in residence at Hammersmith and West London College to devise a show with their students. With our close friends at Contact we are beginning the process for a new show called *Twilight*, for 2007. In November we will be co-hosting the second *European Urban Theatre Festival* in Manchester, where we will also run the fourth *Live and Direct* course in December. Whilst all this is happening **NITRO** is working again at the Royal Opera House for *A NITRO At The Opera 2* and developing our own next major stage show, *The Wedding Dance*, a Salsa Musical, with music by award winning Salsa composer Alex Wilson, and choreography by Deborah Michaels, star of *Chicago* and international Salsa dancer.

Staff
Felix Cross, Artistic Director
Sophia Davidson, Project Manager
Sarah Moore, Freelance Bookkeeper

Board members
Baroness Lola Young
David Emerson
Deborah Williams
Matthew Jones
Alistair Davis

Registered company no: 394673114
NITRO, 6 Brewery Road, London N7 9NH
T: 020 7609 1331
F: 020 7609 1221
E:info@nitro.co.uk
W: www.nitro.co.uk

Please log on to www.nitro.co.uk to subscribe to our e-bulletin or to obtain more information on previous productions.

Production Credits

Costume Supervisor	Isolde Walker
Wardrobe Mistress	Emma Presland
Dresser	Nikki Whitlock
Make Up Artist	Toni Neve
Mr Straker's Make Up designed by	Yasmin Pettigrew
Stage Manager Placement Student	Angie Cadogan
Followspot	Phil Emerson
Production Electrician	Dan Lloyd
Stage Crew	Paul Allen, Glen Neil, Ron Hardman, Dave Munday
Scenery built and painted by	Capital Scenery Limited

We would like to thank: Adrian Reid, Josef Muller, Helmer Hilwig, Bernard Hazell, Maurice Gleeson and Michael Zimmerman.

For *The Big Life*: Enco Products Limited and Honey Rose Herbal Cigarettes.

Theatre Royal Stratford East Staff

Artistic

Artistic Director	Kerry Michael
Associate Director	Dawn Reid
New Writing Manager	Ashmeed Sohoye
Assistant to Artistic Director	Katja Janus
Writer In Residence	Hope Massiah
Senior Script Associate	Myra Brenner
Theatre Archivist	Murray Melvin
Assistant Archivist	Mary Ling

Musical Theatre Project

Associate Director	ULTZ
Associate Artists	Fred Carl, Clint Dyer, Suzanne Gorman, Robert Lee, Paulette Randall, Deborah Sathe, Zoe Simpson

Administration

Administrative Director	Belinda Kidd
Administration Manager	Karen Fisher
Development Director	Elizabeth Royston
Development Consultant	Dilshani Weerasinghe
Finance Manager	Paul Canova
Finance Officer	Elinor Jones

Education
Head of Education Jan Sharkey-Dodds
Youth and Education Officer Karlos Coleman

Marketing And Press
Head of Marketing and Sales Barry Burke
Marketing Officer Silvia Pilotto
Press Officer Michael Siva
Audience Development Manager Kilian Gideon
Box Office Manager Beryl Warner
Box Office Assistants Lucy Atkinson, Asha Bhatti, Davina
Campbell, Alice Cook, Sharleen Fulgence,
Saif Osmani, Sarah Wheeler
Photography Johnny Munday

Technical
Production Manager Chris Robinson
Head of Stage Ben Ranner
Stage Manager Justine Skinner
Deputy Stage Manager on the book Roshni Savjani
Deputy Stage Manager Kala Simpson-Njie
Assistant Stage Manager Altan Reyman
Chief Electrician Stuart Saunders
Deputy Chief Electrician Dave Karley
Assistant Technician Helen Atkinson
Wardrobe Supervisor Isolde Walker

Front of House
Theatre Manager Terry O'Dwyer
Duty Manager Sharleen Fulgence, Lynsey Webb
Maintenance Daniel Harty
Bar Manager Graeme Bright
Bar Assistants Dee Doyin Akinola, Christopher Anipole,
Lukasz Bil, Dawn Dunn, John Karley,
Cristiana Kiki, Piotr Klaczek, Virginia
Kouadio, Kemisha Plummer, Tomas
Sgubin, Ysanne Tidd
Domestic Assistants Julie Lee, Helen Mepham, Magdalena
Sobczynska, Jane Young, Lynsey Webb
Fire Marshals Kofi Agyemang, Daniel Harty, Rameeka
Parvez, Lynsey Webb
Ushers Kofi Agyemang, Emma Ballard, Doreen
Friend, Sonia Gittens, James Gray, Rasmiia
Hazel, Rebecca Howell, Avita Jay, Ashley
Marquis, Noshid Miah, Liz Okinda, Sade
Olokodana, Rameeka Parvez, Jessie
Rawlinson, David Rush, Jalil Saheeb,
Magdalena Sobcynska, Katy Winterflood

Theatre Royal
STRATFORD EAST
'a pioneering theatre' New York Times

Contacting the Theatre

Theatre Royal Stratford East
Gerry Raffles Square
Stratford
London
E15 1BN

Box Office   020 8534 0310
Administration   020 8534 7374
Fax   020 8534 8381
Minicom   020 8279 1114
Press Direct Line   020 8279 1123
Education Direct Line   020 8279 1107

e-mail   theatreroyal@stratfordeast.com
Website   www.stratfordeast.com

Offices opens	Mon – Fri	10am – 6pm
Box Office opens	Mon – Sat	10am – 7pm
Bar opens	Mon – Sat	11am – 11pm
	Sunday	12am – 10.30pm
Food served	Mon – Fri	12am – 2.30pm & 5pm – 7.30pm
	Sunday	12am – 7pm

Caribbean Flavours in the Theatre Royal Bar

The finest fish and chicken spiced and cooked to perfection by our chef, Wills, as well as a wide range of non-Caribbean food, salads and snacks. Now available in the Theatre Royal Bar. Contact the bar at 020 8279 1161.

Thanks to the supporters of the Theatre Royal

We thank the major supporters of Theatre Royal Stratford East for their continuing support: Arts Council England, London Borough of Newham, the Association of London Government and Channel 4 to support our work to develop new musicals.

We would also like to thanks the Funders and Supporters of Theatre Royal Stratford East: Bridge House Estates Trust Fund, Calouste Gulbenkian Foundation, Cultural Industries Development Agency, Clothworkers Build, Equity Trust Fund, European Social Fund, Financial Services Authority, The Foundation for Sport and the Arts, Help a London Child, Jack Petchey Foundation, Ken Hill Trust, Mackintosh Foundation, Mercers' Company, PRS Foundation, Pidem Fund, UBS Investment Bank and Unity Theatre Trust

HIGH HEEL PARROTFISH!

First published in 2005 by Oberon Books Ltd
521 Caledonian Road, London N7 9RH
Tel: 020 7607 3637 / Fax: 020 7607 3629
e-mail: oberon.books@btinternet.com
www.oberonbooks.com

A catalogue record for this book is available from the British
Library.

ISBN: 1 84002 565 4

Cover design by Luke Wakeman
Photography: Michele Martinoli

Printed in Great Britain by Antony Rowe Ltd, Chippenham

Characters

LUCY CHILD

A butch boy with an unholy fascination for drag. Lucy is a close friend of Vashti.

VASHTI KUNARI

A young queen of East Indian origin of about Betty's age. She's from quiet, rural Trinidad.

JUANA LA VENEZOLANA

A Latin firecracker with a heavy Spanish accent and a deeply veiled anger. An old friend of Kitty who falls some ways short of Kitty's refinement.

KITTY CARESS

The grand lady of drag. A faded beauty bearing the star-like elegance of a former era (50-something). When she performs it is clear why she is still revered.

SUZY

The 50 year old ex-drag host(ess). He wears a casual male suit with a generous splash of lipstick.

BETTY BOO

This is the one to watch – the new star in the drag universe. A high energy queen in late teens or early twenties set to inherit Kitty's throne.

LEANDRA

The mystery woman…

Stage

The stage simulates a cabaret stage. There is a velvet curtain, in front of which Suzy talks to the audience. The girls also perform there. This curtain then rises to reveal the cluttered backstage dressing room where the girls sit side by side behind a long table.

Place/Time

Miss Miller's Bar – A seedy night-club in Trinidad. The play is in real time.

Costumes

Backstage:	Dressing gowns.
In performance:	Big, grand – Rio Carnival Style. They are practically the sets of the show.

ACT 1

Lights come up on a 'Welcome to Trinidad' billboard. KITTY, JUANA, VASHTI and LUCY stand in front in a fantasy scene.

LUCY: You feeling the heat?

VASHTI: Yes, I feeling the heat.

JUANA: And how it feeling?

KITTY: What you think? Sweet!

Song 1
Sung by LUCY, JUANA, KITTY and VASHTI

SUZY enters in a joyous explosion.

SUZY: Hello everyone and welcome to the first ever drag cabaret in Miss Miller's bar, Port of Spain...

The spotlight comes on him and dazes him like a deer in headlights. He looks at himself in alarm...

Wrong foundation. Fashion Mistake!

SUZY runs off the stage in a fright.

The billboard begins to topple on the others.

LUCY / VASHTI / JUANA / KITTY: Aahhhhh!

They go dark as SUZY returns nervously to the stage with the spotlight on her.

SUZY: Hello everyone and welcome to Miss Miller's bar right here in Port of Spain and this island's first ever daring show called 'Sparkle, Sparkle'. I have it in my script to ask you to make some noise so make some noise please. Thank you. Sorry about running off the stage earlier but nobody warned me we had a spotlight...

35

Hold on… (*Shouting to the spotlight.*) Up there! Turn it down! I ain't wear the colour scheme for that! Hello! (*Nothing happens.*) Anyway, I'm glad so many of you risked coming. As you know, tonight is dedicated to larger-than-life Able Mabel who was last seen being bitch-slapped into a police van and is now dead. She always considered herself a showgirl so we thought if butch men could squeeze in a dress on Carnival day and bend-foot-gyal could prance in feathers, it's time we make a rumble too. And babies, what a rumble! I have five international beauties with more legs than a crab! Ready to start the jam?!… No, wait. I have it in my script to say hello to the tourists first…like you. You look first world…ooh my, you well buff. What's your name? Here for the Carnival? Who you with, (*Pointing to someone else.*) that bitch? You had to be with one of the locals to get in here and yes you's a bitch because you pass me straight in the road last week – to hide your story. Honey, your story in your mince. Anyway, I hope he tell you to pack court clothes as our lifestyle could land you before a magistrate. If the police raid us, run. But enjoy the show. As for the rest of you, remember this is supposed to be a Members' Only Sport Association. Talk cricket and football when you outside. It might be Carnival Friday but the neighbours can still sniff us out. Enough of that now. It's time to hit the alternative side of Carnival running. These dolls have been practising hard for five weeks to get it right for you and Mabel. So without further ado, let's mash up the place. Make some noise for the brave, the incomparable – Carnival Barbies!

No one enters.

(*Hopefully.*) Carnival Barbies…? Somebody please say they didn't leave me out here alone. No really – tell me we're not running on Caribbean time.

A light brightens on LUCY backstage. The others are hustling to get ready in dimmer light. LUCY sings slowly.

SONG 2
Sung by LUCY

Lights brighten on all. KITTY is in despair.

JUANA: We missed the cue.

LUCY: I don't care 'bout that. Show me what to do with this make-up thing.

VASHTI: If I go any faster I'll paint out me eye.

JUANA: Kitty, move it. We have to be out there NOW!

KITTY: Tell Suzy to stop hosting. Betty didn't show. The entire night cancelled.

Back to SUZY.

SUZY: Look at you and look at me. You feeling nice?… Nice. We'll be all right. Something will happen – eventually…

LUCY: Tell me what to do or I'll get rough on somebody!

VASHTI: Honey, you don't need any more.

KITTY: Keep that gangsta behaviour outside, eh. I told you before you're with ho's, not your homies… Why did I put this night together?

JUANA: You get too big for your corset. You forget what happen to Mabel.

KITTY: It was making a stand for Mabel that I was thinking about.

JUANA: No chica, you dying long time to impress the whole scene. Well, the scene reach and they not impressed. Slap your face on for the first number and forget Betty.

KITTY: But Meryl Stripper and Barbara Stretchole out there. They will laugh at us. My choreography was made for five.

JUANA: That's all? I'm built for ten, give or take two either way.

VASHTI: Miss Kitty, you sure it's not nerves?

KITTY: Nerves? Did this country wench ask me if I have nerves?

LUCY: Vashti right. You been rehearsing us this way and that till we late, Kitty. The President ain't coming.

KITTY: *MISS* Kitty. There's a hierarchy here and you're the newcomer.

JUANA: (*Gently.*) Come on, Kitty. I know you're worried but this is what we promised.

KITTY: Juana, it's our first time ever. I need Betty to cover that clumsy, butch bitch…I mean that in love, eh.

JUANA: Mira mija, all of town hot tonight with Carnival. I wanted to give my sugar daddy his heart pills and be in a party instead of risking a bashing here…/

LUCY: Until somebody in the party grab you down below.

VASHTI: And I could a been lock up in the village with Ma and Pa – until they go to bed and I sneak off.

LUCY: And I ready to wine up on a gyal instead of trying to look like one, but nobody helping me!

JUANA / VASHTI / LUCY: And what about Suzy?

SUZY: You know what? I think I will take a little break and come back again.

SUZY exits.

38

JUANA: That's it. Action time. (*To LUCY.*) Bring your face. Blusher left. Imagine you're biting a lime.

LUCY: Eh? Man, I will pump four bullets in anybody chest who try forcin' me.

JUANA: Vashti, take over on your bandit friend and hurry.

LUCY: I tell you don't repeat that bandit talk round here. Vashti, you know I wouldn't watch a lime and...

VASHTI: BITE THE BLASTED LIME!... Looks like I nervous too.

LUCY squints and VASHTI blushes his cheeks.

Take it easy, Lucas... I mean Lucy. We only have to get through tonight and we break for freedom. Act like a lady if you want it.

JUANA: Let's do what we're here for, cariòas. Adios, Kitty.

KITTY rushes and blocks the exit.

KITTY: Girls, no. We bow out now so they don't talk us bad. Yes, I'm nervous. I told everyone I could do this. Juana, you know I'm a danseur and a choreographer...

JUANA: Honey, you're a dental nurse.

KITTY: My mother had me trained in ballet and jazz and nobody believes it. If only I could make mama proud. But she's in a sick bed and Betty's probably in somebody else's bed so let's go home.

LUCY: Kitty move. I catching a cramp in me calf.

KITTY: *Miss* Kitty. If these gutless queens weren't scared of exposure I wouldn't be saddled with you....Oh God, palpitations. Water, Juana.

JUANA: Just step over her and let's go.

39

KITTY: You all deaf? It's off. Nobody going in or out unless it's through me….Ooh, more palpitations. Juana, help or I die…

SUZY pushes through KITTY from the other side. The spotlight is still on him.

SUZY: What going on here? I'm in front sweating gravy and you all in the back chatting?

KITTY: (*In horror.*) Suzy, what's wrong? You're off colour. What happened? Didn't he come?

LUCY: (*In disgust.*) He? Uggh…

SUZY: I don't know. I can't see past the fifth row, and stop minding my business!… Thanks for telling me we found a spotlight, Kitty.

KITTY: You know we put the word out, and a guy turned up last minute. He was ready to chance losing his reputation for money.

SUZY: Sweetheart, everybody chancing more than their reputation to come and not be able to run. But they come. We doing it or not?

JUANA: She back out. She waiting for Betty.

SUZY: Look Kitty, I left this life behind long ago but you twisted me arm like you twisted every closeted carnival designer arm to get your commemoration night. I'm here with that much script. So get your arse out and bring down the house. Everybody to the storeroom and get into costumes now, and pull them higher up the batty line! If I have to go down tonight it won't be in shame.

KITTY: But…but…/

SUZY: And you will show leg in front in two minutes or I'll announce your age to the bar.

KITTY: Hurry, dearies!

SUZY: Sorry to be tough, Kitty, but I invited someone. We go to the wire. Don't miss the cue.

JUANA: You have money, Suzy. You should have put a monitor back here. Oh, you forgot to introduce yourself at the top. No one knows who or what you are.

SUZY exits.

We need to pray to our Lord Jesu Cristo for success. Gather round.

VASHTI: But I'm a Hindu.

KITTY: Forget prayers. We have to think about being fabulous without Betty. I'm worried about Suzy. She look bad, eh.

All exit. SUZY enters downstage to the audience (with spotlight).

SUZY: Okay, hold on to your wigs. We're doing it for real now. By the way, my name is Suzy. I'm the old guy who usually sits alone at the far end of the bar. I gave up this apparel fifteen years ago but tonight I've come out of retirement and only God knows why. Anyway, we're here to have a good time so let's do it. Ladies and gentlemen, the Carnival Barbies!

The music goes up in tempo. The girls enter in 'very high cut' carnival costumes with feathers, beads etc. Rio carnival style.

KITTY: I'm Kitty!

JUANA: I'm Juana!

VASHTI: I'm Vashti.

LUCY: (*Butchly.*) I'm Lucy.

KITTY: Take it up an octave, love!

Song 3
Sung by KITTY, JUANA, VASHTI, LUCY (and BETTY)

BETTY enters in the musical bridge.

BETTY: (*High pitched scream.*) Hellooo!

JUANA: She reach at the wrong time!

KITTY: Pssst – Betty. Stay to the back. I changed the steps.

BETTY: No way, sugar. I'm the star. Stand behind me!

The girls do individual parades but BETTY determinedly steps forward to do hers. KITTY and JUANA step in front and blot her out.

VASHTI: (*To LUCY.*) There'll be blood in the house tonight.

The girls exit. SUZY enters.

SUZY: Whooeee! The Carnival Barbies, boys and girls! We're packing with steam! Now, they're going to change, come back one by one and I'll entertain you with chat in between. I want to start with fashion. I know it's Carnival country and we like bright colours but you people here like your colours with an expensive label. Why? (*To someone in the audience.*) Look at you – in MTV gear but probably with no food on your table. I don't mind but my sisters can't walk into town and buy a label yet you laugh when you see us somewhere. So, let's investigate this schism…if I can see. I swear this lightman work in the airport tower. You sir, who dressed you?… All right. You ever try heels? You ever try anyone in heels? Forget the consumerism. I'll teach you what drag queens have learnt for island dressing. Suzy's five essential fashion tips! Go for legroom coz when these natives on to you, labels trap air and slow the get away. If Mabel didn't import a tight Gucci skirt she would've been here today. So don't laugh at the sisters cause we all in the same boat. But looking at this lovely lady here, I'm ready to give fashion tip number two coz I see a survival error happening. Are you ready, ma'am…?

Lights out sharply on SUZY and rise backstage. Everyone but BETTY is in a good mood. LUCY is readying to go to the costume room.

BETTY: What went on? I always lead the chorus.

KITTY: You were late, honey bunch.

BETTY: I do work. These looks have to be paid for.

JUANA: That cheap Penny Mart is work? I thought it was slavery.

BETTY: Darling, I don't fool a sugar daddy to…/

KITTY: Betty, relax! We have to think about who's next.

BETTY: Madam, you never said anything to that stale fajita (*JUANA.*) when she missed almost every rehearsal.

JUANA: But I caught the show. Always a bride – never a bridesmaid.

VASHTI: You were good out there, Lucy. Remember to breathe when you go back on.

BETTY: I'm too gorgeous for this. You let Juana off because she's your best friend. You didn't even ask why I was late. I was chased by…

VASHTI: (*Panicked.*) Chased?! Forget going back on, Lucy. Pack your things.

BETTY: No, fool. I mean I was chased by…

KITTY: Betty, that's past! We excited them. Anybody noticed Meryl and Barbara?

JUANA: Envy in their throats. I also noticed someone looking at me for a salsa dip. Betty, noticed anyone? Oh no, you didn't make it to the front line.

BETTY: I'm not taking this, you see.

KITTY: For God's sake, you'll get your turn. Calm down.

LUCY: I going now, Kitty. I'll bust them up.

KITTY: *Miss* Kitty. You're a goldfish? Wait, love…ahm… Juana, you tell her.

JUANA: Me? I don't want to get shot.

KITTY: Lucy honey, I know you're going to be disappointed but I made an executive decision. I want Vashti now. Vashti, go, go, go!

LUCY: But we rehearse me going first to get me out the way.

KITTY: I know but it's different. Barbara and Meryl Stripper out there. It's not just them. We were better than I expected. I want to keep the fire up. You understand.

LUCY: But I work harder than anyone else because I don't live like you all.

KITTY: We'll pay you, honey. But this is our thing. Vashti, go now. Betty, stop sulking. You're using up the oxygen in the room and it's hot enough already.

LUCY: Vashti, you knew she was pulling me?

VASHTI: No.

BETTY: Sabotage. I'll tell Suzy.

KITTY: Girls, look up. We're going great. Miss Miller arranged a special treat for you at the bar so everyone can touch you. Juana, you and I will celebrate at the Cabinet Minister's house – very discreet, very posh. His wife in New York. (*To all.*) See? We're becoming the hottest things in town.

LUCY: But nobody will see me and I practise all out.

KITTY: What's your problem, Lucy? On any other night you and your roughneck crew would be stoning us and we'd be answering with bottles. Sit down.

LUCY: But I ain't with them. They're out for my head and if they see me like this I even more dead. All I been doing is killing myself to get my song right, singing loud in the night for the past week.

VASHTI: I know, baby. I was worried Pa would hear you.

JUANA: He's at yours now?

LUCY: Tie up in a cowshed with half dead cows to stay low, and still I was going at it.

KITTY: Honey, I'm feeling existential so let me put it to you in butch terms. You're one of them things in football that you call a reserve…

JUANA: A substitute, mija. I watch footballers – I mean football.

KITTY: Whatever it is, you come if everyone dies. Vashti, move.

LUCY: That ain't good enough. I in a panic whole week. I deserve my chance. You want me mash up the place?

KITTY: Sugar dumpling, you want to alert the neighbours? We have the whole night to get through. Don't make me reach for the pepper spray in my handbag.

VASHTI: Miss Kitty, please, don't. Lucy's my friend. I'll have to grab the six-inch Rambo knife from my beauty case.

KITTY: Really? How you going to find it with pepper spray in your eyes, dear?

VASHTI: How you going to spray with no hands, love?

JUANA: How long they going to keep you all out the armed forces, darlings? Suzy is about to run out of script. Make a decision.

KITTY: Vashti, Lucy, please, it's for the best. This is not one of your country dives where drunken farm boys will take a clumsy bitch like Lucy. Lucy, I mean that in friendship. This is the city, and them people oppressed, vex and ready to boo – like us. Hear what. Vashti, you go now, soften them and Lucy you'll follow later. Understand?

LUCY: (*Grudgingly.*) Go on, Vashti. Grab your things.

KITTY: Thank God. I'm sweating. I wish Millie had put a fan in for us hoes.

JUANA: Betty, spread your legs. We need a wind.

VASHTI: Better tie down the table first.

All but BETTY laugh.

KITTY: Come on, Betty; you'll be fabulous when you go out. You want to come to the Minister's with us after? He likes you. Smile.

JUANA: It would help if she take her teeth out her arse and put it in her mouth.

KITTY: (*Laughing.*) Stop please. My facelift stitches will snap.

BETTY: Well, well, here I was thinking we were fighting a noble cause. But you two really out to big up yourself over everybody. I'm changing that. I'm going now.

KITTY: Eh? I warned Suzy in advance about switching Lucy – not you.

LUCY: Thanks. So, you had it planned for me long time?

46

BETTY: You might have blotted me out on stage, Miss Girl, but you can't blot this…

BETTY pulls out a large portrait photo of herself and hangs it on the wall.

Look and worship, sluts. $20.99 at the Photo Shop and they didn't even recognise it was me. I'm ahead now.

JUANA: (*Looking at the portrait in fear.*) It's staring at me.

VASHTI: Me too. I feel dirty.

KITTY: Betty, behave…

BETTY: Honey, all week I've been facing bitches at the make-up counter buying Carnival make-up and pointing their fingers at me, and I've been thinking I'll get me own back tonight. We promised to work together for that. But you spoilt it. I'm not waiting anymore.

JUANA: I knew she was going to do something stupid soon enough. It's her nature.

BETTY: As for you, Kitty let the cat out. I know why you were missing rehearsals.

JUANA: (*Nervously.*) What does she mean by that, Kitty?

KITTY: Nothing… Betty, please. You'll mess it up.

BETTY: I've gone deaf now, Old Bat. It's every beauty for herself. Do you know how long I've been waiting to be seen by a real audience?

LUCY: No.

BETTY: Don't interrupt me… Only one can win this race and it's time they know who.

VASHTI: It's still staring at me.

The music starts and the girls become BETTY's stagehands and dress her. Lights brighten on SUZY down centre fanning herself nervously.

SUZY: That was my last fashion tip and it looks like we hit another delay. Don't think it's a reason to start eyeing up each other. I'm still here. What I will do is take the opportunity to thank a special friend who I hope made it tonight. Don't worry; I'm not going to call your name in public. With this bunch it's like scrawling it in the toilet.… He doesn't like the dressing-up business – especially on me. I better stop here before he walks out. Ahmm… I don't want to move on in the script. You want a joke? Knock, knock. (*He shoves the mike at someone.*) … Nobody knocks anymore, sugar. We have doorbells in the Caribbean. Ahm, how about some music? Millie, go on the system while I check our friends backstage! Oh wait. I'm getting a signal. Thank God… Yes, it's time to bring on the first solo performer…

BETTY enters directly from the dressing room to front stage.

SUZY: Ladies and gentlemen, please welcome the devil in the works, the spice in your curry – Miss Vashti…. Betty? Where you come from?

BETTY: Me mother. Now, play my music!

SUZY exits.

Song 4
Sung by BETTY

BETTY bows and exits as SUZY enters confused.

SUZY: Betty Boo, ladies and gentlemen. I was supposed to tell you that Betty is the best of the next generation but she came in the wrong… Give me a minute. (*SUZY shouts directly to KITTY. Lights brighten on KITTY in the dressing room.*) Kitty!!

KITTY: Aargh! You're still off colour.

SUZY: Look, tell me who's next.

KITTY: I need to get everyone back to calm before we move on. I'll give you a sign.

SUZY: How can I work the script if I don't know who's coming?

KITTY: Fluff about and be camp. Charm them. Just say anything.

Lights go out on KITTY. SUZY turns to the audience.

SUZY: (*Laughing uncomfortably.*) Heh, heh… We going good, eh? You having a nice time? Nice. Well, I could talk about lifestyles but that was supposed to go with Betty. Does anybody have any topic they feel they'd like to discuss here for a few minutes? How about you, sir? You have anything sensible to get off your well-endowed chest?… Hold it, love. Don't look panicked. I only want talk and nothing more. Nothing of my stature comes cheap. I'm a tax-paying adult with a solid reputation. I have house, car and a big son at university… Oh shit. I wasn't supposed to mention I'm a breeder. Rewind!

Black out on SUZY. Backstage brightens. BETTY hasn't returned yet.

KITTY: Remember where we are and what we're doing. Let's go over the mantra…love, love, love… (*To JUANA.*) Is that Betty bitch finished changing in the storeroom?

JUANA: No.

KITTY: Love, love, love – are we feeling it? I don't know what happened to her. She feels that kicking up her heels is all it takes to win a crowd. I could teach her different.

VASHTI: (*Teasing.*) But Miss Kitty, I hear in your day your heels were always in the air. I hear they used to call you rocket heels – press your button and lift off.

KITTY: At least I have heels that fit – unlike your big foot friend. Love, love, love.

LUCY: How I come in that? (*To VASHTI.*) I thought you all were nice, funny people.

VASHTI: Who fooled you? Crabs in a barrel, babe. They will climb over each other to get out.

JUANA: That makes you a crab as well.

VASHTI: No dear, I'm half out. Once Miss Kitty pays us for tonight, Lucy and me making the final instalment on a plane ticket and flying off this damn rock. We're going to the US to be treated like proper people.

KITTY: Where you're going is on that stage. Hit the storeroom and shove Betty aside. We can't wait anymore.

LUCY: I don't know, Vashti. I ain't so sure 'bout leaving.

VASHTI: What? You mad? We have it planned.

KITTY: I want you singing now. That's the plan…

VASHTI: I announced it to Ma and Pa. They're still crying their eyes out. You can't back out now.

LUCY: What's the point? If I can't do anything here, what I going to do there?

JUANA: You're right, mija.

KITTY: Doesn't anybody listen to me?

VASHTI: How long you intend to live in the cowshed? Your posse and the police looking for you. Sooner or later Pa will find you. Wake up: it's only one way left.

LUCY: Look at me. You all can't stop laughing when I walk in heels. Kitty promised to let me on next and she still sending you because I ain't good enough. I'm hanging with drag queens, and I still can't make the grade.

VASHTI: Fine, Lucy. You stay and take it. I'm making my way. I fed up of the boys in the village calling me chi-chi man by day and trying to hold me hand at night. I'm going on stage, make my money and never look back. Stay and end up with a police bullet in your head.

KITTY: That's it – stop! I finally know why we're having problems tonight. It's a bad spirit. Somebody brought a bad spirit back here.

JUANA: It's in the storeroom, cariòa.

KITTY: I can feel it. It's around. We have to get rid of it before we move on.

VASHTI: Miss Kitty, Suzy…

KITTY: Forget Suzy. We're not going to make any headway. The last time I felt a bad spirit my Auntie Probity fell and broke her hip.

JUANA: For God's sake, Kitty – not your voodoo again.

KITTY: Shoo away, bad spirit! Shoo! Vashti, you're too young to have such negative thoughts. Tonight, we're trying to make a difference. Forget lining up for any damn visa. It's all the bad vibes from the police, them haters and even inside you that the spirit working on. Come on girls, we need to glitter in our minds!

VASHTI: What?

JUANA: Glitter in your mind. That's how she does it. The first time I met Kitty she was lying drunk in a drain downtown on Carnival Tuesday, and she was still glittering.

KITTY: Not that story, Juana. I'm a local legend.

JUANA: I know what I'm doing. Anyway, Kitty was a young glamour puss, a silver screen star from the posh side of town. I had just arrived in the country, didn't know anyone and didn't want to give myself away. So, I played Carnival in a butch band called 'O Africa'. I was a Zulu warrior with a red satin cape I added myself, and lots and lots of bright green ostrich feathers that caught the sun in a fantasia. No one suspected I was a queen.

KITTY: Move it on, please.

JUANA: While I'm pretending to be Shaka Zulu, I see Kitty lying there, dress torn, wig shifted and ordering a rum bottle to find her mouth. I looked at her; she looked at me and said: 'Darling, do you have a straw? I'm smudging my lipstick.' I knew I'd come home.

KITTY: Glitter in your minds, children. We can't let people get to us. I'll show you.

Song 5
Sung by KITTY, VASHTI and JUANA. They create a fantasy beauty pageant.

The girls laugh and high-five each other. LUCY rushes to make a contribution.

LUCY: Once upon a time a man said to me.
'Boy, like you ain't realise you's the bling-blingest pimp them ho's ever…'

KITTY: Honey no! Not you. Vashti, ready now?

VASHTI: Yes, Ma'am.

KITTY: Suzy?! Suzy honey, are you all right?

Lights brighten on SUZY chatting to the audience.

SUZY: No. I told them I have a pickney and they want to know how. Help.

KITTY: Vashti will be there in two minutes. Bye.

Light out on SUZY. BETTY enters backstage as VASHTI exits.

BETTY: Did you hear them? They loved me! I'm on a cloud! I wish I could travel the world and live on applause.

KITTY: We love you too, Betty. We want you to know it. Say it, girls…

JUANA: Don't overdo it, Kitty. You must've been sniffing the cheap make-up she sells at the Penny Mart.

BETTY: And here I was ready to forgive everything, but there's always a stale taco to spoil the fun. Don't ruin it, babe. I mean, I could mention that I know while we were sweating it out at rehearsals you were running off to church to pray, but I wouldn't. Oops, sorry Kitty. I forgot you said it was a secret.

JUANA: I knew you let it out! I said no one is to know!

KITTY: Me? I can't remember.

BETTY: Can you believe it? Of all of us here, she's the only one mad enough to walk around like that 24/7 and she still has a spot on her conscience. I hope you prayed for talent – but God has limits. Let me hear you agree, Lucy.

JUANA: You told them all!

KITTY: I really can't remember. Betty, sit down. We don't want need that now.

BETTY: Actually Kitty, now that I'm top draw I think I'm ready to take that throne. Pack up your chins and sit next to Joan of Arc.

KITTY: Love, love – look love; don't get stupid or I'll give you the throne where no one can retrieve it. What's wrong with you tonight?

BETTY: You've been messing around with me too long.

JUANA: Just slap her, Kitty. Oops – did I say that? Sorry Betty. I shouldn't have mentioned that I know last Christmas you were slapped in the square by an accidental tourist for misrepresenting your gender. I heard he left you drinking soup for a week.

BETTY: (*To KITTY.*) You told her?!

KITTY: Me? I can't remember.

BETTY: It was a secret.

JUANA: She told us all.

BETTY: How could you? No more games. You two bitches need to come down!

JUANA: No honey, you're coming down!

LUCY: For God's sake, shut up! Vashti is on next! Keep quiet.

KITTY: (*In shock.*) Did she just raise her voice at us?

BETTY: You're the newcomer.

JUANA: You don't speak to Betty that way. Sit down.

BETTY: Thank you. They have no manners these days.

KITTY: Now where were we?

BETTY: I was about to take you down.

JUANA: No love, I'm taking you down!

JUANA grabs BETTY's picture and aims for a hat stand.

KITTY: Juana, wait!

JUANA impales it.

My God, you didn't have to go that far.

JUANA: A wooden stake through the heart and she's still alive. Better switch to a silver bullet. (*Deadly serious.*) Don't mess with me. It'll be you and not a picture next time.

BETTY: (*Very hurt.*) I was taking it as a joke all along. But you really want to go for me. You'll see what you stirred up, Mother Teresa. You'll regret it.

BETTY exits.

KITTY: This doesn't mean anything. We're all relating. That's good. The glass is half full.

Lights out backstage and brighten on an uncomfortable SUZY downstage.

SUZY: Why am I feeling put on the spot for having a son? Come on; we've all done things for society. You know what this place is like. I don't mean my son was for society. He came out of the marriage… Oh Lord, I'm making it worse. Yes, I was married, but I'm divorced. Officially, I'm divorced but she's still in me tail. Look, my special friend doesn't need to hear this. The talk ends here. If you want to gossip then say I'm capable of many things. Don't let the clothes fool you. They certainly didn't fool my ex-wife. Up next is Vashti Kunari. Vashti, hurry please!… So, if I can get back to the fashion tip that was supposed to go with Vashti, ethnic wear is a must-have for…

BETTY enters and crosses over to the band.

SUZY: Betty? You again?

BETTY: I want to get to the other end of this shit hole. The Bollywood reject ready. Take a second look folks. I'm still fierce.

SUZY: Betty Boo, ladies and gentlemen. No one crosses a stage like her. You heard. It's Vashti. I like her a lot. She's a small girl with big dreams. And those are hard to hold on to in tropical heat. Please welcome the devil in the works, the spice in your curry – Miss Vashti Kunari.

VASHTI appears as a proper Bollywood girl.

Song 6
Sung by VASHTI

BETTY crosses back while VASHTI notices someone in the audience and leans over the stage to take a closer look. She suddenly screams and runs off the stage before her next verse. SUZY enters.

SUZY: All right, this ain't working. It ain't working. We're trying to do something for you but it's too tough. Who scared Vashti? Come on, which one of you? What wrong with you all? Hear nah, we're not professionals at this. We're only trying to stir a little pride in the house and raise the tone. The least you could do is respect it. I'm going to ask Vashti to come again and you all had better behave. We're going to start over. I mean completely start over and get this thing right. And this time I'm doing it without any light. Turn that thing off!

The spotlight remains on SUZY. Backstage brightens as VASHTI enters in terror. SUZY eventually walks off stage with the spotlight following her.

LUCY: What happened?

JUANA: Talk chica, what is it?

VASHTI: Out there…! Him!

KITTY: Who?

VASHTI points and garbles and runs about the room in panic.

JUANA: She's making me nervous, Kitty.

KITTY: This bad spirit won't be beat.

BETTY: Move aside.

BETTY grabs hold of VASHTI and slaps her. VASHTI becomes even more hysterical.

JUANA: Nice shot. I respect that.

BETTY: It works better on TV though. Better try again.

KITTY: Someone get her to talk or I'll resort to pepper spray.

LUCY: Vashti, your sari have a rip!!

VASHTI: (*Suddenly serious.*) Where?

LUCY: What happened?

VASHTI: Me neighbour, Mr Rampaul, I just saw him.

BETTY: That's it?

VASHTI: He going to out me to my parents. He did it before. Pa will kill me dead.

BETTY: Anybody notice anything odd about that sentence? He did it before? Honey, you get to come out once.

KITTY: How dare you hold us up for that? Lucy, you go. I should've sent you in the first place.

VASHTI: You can't! He knows you too.

LUCY: I'm not going to give up my spot for something you imagined. You always seeing that man everywhere.

VASHTI: Because he dragged me out in front the village. He caught me like this one night sneaking into a taxi. He grab me from behind, pull me back and call everyone out to see. Pa break down in tears. It took six men to stop him strangling me. It's only because I promised never to do it again and say I was mad that he didn't throw me out. I can't get caught again. I have to go home!

KITTY: I don't think so, sweetie. You signed up for three songs. You'll have to deal.

SUZY enters spotlit.

SUZY: What happened, Vashti? You all right?

KITTY: She *thinks* she saw her neighbour, Mr Rampaul. He wants to out her – again.

VASHTI: I have to get home before he tells Pa. I'll be on crutches for the rest of my life.

SUZY: All right, go.

KITTY: What?! You mad?! She has to sing.

SUZY: Don't play you don't know what it's like, Kitty. Nobody going to step in and take the blows for her. Most of Trinidad will applaud. That's why I hang up my heels and I'm not going back. In this place only one person has to know your secret and your life finished. We'll work around her. Send someone else.

VASHTI: Send? There's no more sending. The show is over.

JUANA: What you mean?

VASHTI: You don't know Mr Rampaul. That man believes God put him on earth to get rid of sickos like us. He will call the police. He'll have the place crawling with cops. Lucy, tell them.

KITTY: Keep quiet, Lucy. It's reserve time. You go on and don't fall in anybody's lap.

SUZY: Lucy, is it true?

Pause.

LUCY: (*Blurting.*) I can't let the police find me. I'm wanted for attempted armed robbery.

KITTY: Shut up. I told you before not in here. Could you see me appearing in court and giving my man name to the gallery as a witness? Get into costume before I change my mind.

SUZY: Whow, whow, hold on. We have a problem.

KITTY: Of course, we have a problem. Nobody's out front. I will go if you all going to stand around.

SUZY: You told me he was decent. You said he was all right to make up numbers for your routines.

KITTY: He's wearing a panty. How could he be decent? You think I held auditions at the Girl Guides?

LUCY: Stop there! I am decent, all right?! What make you think you know about me? I get caught up in stupidness. I don't have money so I get tie up with a posse. They told me to hold up a hardware store to prove meself. They gave me a gun and told me to shoot the owner in his head if anything went wrong. It went wrong, yes. The man was scared. He pulled my mask off, and I had the gun to his mouth and was thinking: 'Shoot him. He going to report me to the police and I already have nothing.' Only people like you telling me I'm shit. But he was scared. He wasn't trying to be no hero. So you know what I did? I ran – out of the shop and past the posse. Now they all looking for me for something I didn't do. So, don't wash your mouth on me. You don't know the first damn thing 'bout me.

SUZY: All right, Lucy – calm down. Girls, this is more than we can handle. I'm stopping the show here.

KITTY: You're mad! I'm going on…

SUZY: Kitty, sit down! I have a boy out there and I'm not going to risk his neck or mine! Millie's managing to keep this place by a fingernail, and all it takes is one phone call, one police car out front and this neighbourhood will come down on us in a rage. We're doing it for Mabel. We don't want to join her. The show is over.

KITTY: But all this work…and I was saving my song for last…

SUZY: I know you're disappointed but we have no choice. It's what we agreed with Millie – no serious threats. I got partly dressed up for the first time in years too. What I want to know is how the hell Mr Rampaul managed to get in?

VASHTI: He must have used my name at the door.

SUZY: That means the word has spread further than the community. Who else managed to get in? Kitty, it was a grand idea, a fabulous idea, but it's just too much for us. You could see it all evening. I know it is for me. Maybe next year. Girls, pack up and move out fast. I'm giving the signal out front.

BETTY: Can I say one thing? I performed and was adored. I'm queen of the night.

JUANA: Hold it, Suzy. You can't walk out and say 'police raid' to those Toilet Marys. They'll stampede like it's the perfume counter at duty free. You'll have the worst riot for sure. You need an evacuation plan… I know. I'll perform.

SUZY: What?

JUANA: I'm a Christian, darling. I'll sacrifice myself. No one can move or use a cell phone while the show is running. I'll sing and keep Rampaul in his chair. You get

Millie to spread the word to the audience so they leave gently. Vashti, where is Rampaul?

VASHTI: At the back. 5'8", 46 and ¾ year old Indian male with a mole on the left shoulder blade and tight buns. Medium size underwear I think.

They all look at her in awe.

A girl notices things in a crisis.

JUANA: Back out, Suzy, and remain natural.

SUZY: But…

JUANA: Go! Go! We don't have much time!

SUZY exits.

KITTY: (*To JUANA.*) Good work, bitch. I see you managed to squeeze your performance in.

JUANA: I didn't get dressed up for nothing.

KITTY: I'll be on right after. Suzy isn't going to pull the plug on me like that.

LUCY: What about me?

JUANA: Wish me luck, Betty. We'll see who's queen of the night.

JUANA exits. BETTY goes contritely to KITTY.

BETTY: Kitty, a minute. I need to tell you something. It's about Juana. Well, it's something I did to Juana. (*Defensively.*) I didn't know the show was going to close early.

KITTY: Lord – what next?

Lights out backstage. SUZY enters downstage.

SUZY: All right, forget Vashti. She's not coming back. (*Remembering the danger.*) What am I saying? Of course,

61

she is – that is to anyone who's interested, like anyone in the back row, with tight buns. It's all going so good tonight at Miss Miller's I can scream. I think I will! (*In a low voice.*) *SEAN...* Sorry, the name of my special friend slipped out... Sean, I need you to meet me backstage right now. Nothing serious, you all understand. I just want to know if he's enjoying it. Sean, stand up if you're here! Don't be shy! Stand up! Light man, turn the damn thing down! Sean...? (*Very disappointed.*) Well, well, I guess he didn't come. He said he'd give me a try. No sense crying over spilt milk, eh. Let's move on to the next topic of discussion. I don't want to be the only one on the spot so let's talk about kids. How many of us manage to hold down the pervy life in this country with a kid in tow? As I'm telling you it all I might as well say I didn't. Nah man, my darling wife, or Leandra when she's in human form, kicked me out my house, told me to give up the garter and stay away from you folk if I ever wanted to see him again. I've come out of retirement because I thought he'd reached an age where he could think for himself, and he said he'd come tonight. But he didn't bother! Why did I bother hoping?

JUANA: Ay Suzy, estoy lista.

SUZY: Yes... I'm going off script. Ahm, wicked boys and girls get ready for some salsa. This is South America's secret weapon. So hold on to your lightning rod as I call down la tempesta divina... Yes loves, I'm multi lingual. I can do many things with my tongue... Please welcome the divine storm, Juana La Venezolana.

JUANA enters forestage ready to perform a salsa explosion. The playback begins with a cascade of notes as she gears up to explode. To her surprise, an opera aria comes on. She tries to sing along but doesn't know the words. She steps forward angrily and shouts to Millie to go back to the original arrangement.

Song 7
Sung by JUANA

SUZY: You all still here? Millie, didn't you spread the word about our unwanted guest with the tight buns?! New rules – don't move about unless you're leaving and no use of cell phones... Look at me. I'm a bundle of nerves. All I need now is my ex wife to see me and I'll be dead... But to tell the truth... I miss this excitement. Reminds me of a time when...

Lights down on SUZY and up back stage as a ferocious JUANA enters.

JUANA: (*To BETTY.*) Stand back. Her bony arse is mine!

KITTY jumps in the way.

KITTY: Save it for later, Juana. I want to go on. It's my only chance.

LUCY: (*To JUANA.*) Betty has something she wants to say to you.

VASHTI: Betty?

KITTY: I know 'sorry' is the hardest word but just shape your lips into an s.

LUCY: Say it!

VASHTI: Why are we waiting around to sort them out, Lucy? Let's go home.

LUCY: I got dressed up as a girl. I want my chance. Say it, Betty! Say sorry!

BETTY: Sssssssssskanky bitch!

KITTY: Oh Jesus.

JUANA: She is history!

BETTY: All of a sudden you care about how you look? What about the rest of us who put our necks on the block every time we came here to rehearse? You treat this all as a big joke. You're swanning around with your sugar daddy and using up good space in church because you're a blasted foreigner. Our problems don't matter. And you thought I was going to let you off and not give you stick? You want penance? It just start, Sister Bernadette. Go back to your damn country.

JUANA begins unstrapping her shoe.

JUANA: Ay Cinderella, the ball is over but don't leave without your slipper. I'll plant it in your scalp and make it fit.

KITTY: Juana – love, love, love…

BETTY: Let her go. She feel she can bring down the locals. This has been a long time coming.

KITTY: Grow up, Betty. Tonight is just a game. When the police come through that door every man jack out there will run and deny you. There ain't no love anywhere for a drag queen no matter what country she's from. Face the fact and start packing your things.

BETTY: That does not explain Miss Miller's rottweiler attacking me when I was coming up the alley. Somebody set him loose. That wasn't a game. That's why I was late. Who did it, eh?

KITTY: Impossible. Millie would never let anyone touch Periwinkle.

BETTY: It was you, Juana. The heat was on so you tried to get a dog to take me out.

JUANA: Honestly, why would I set a dog on a dog? That's why you got slapped. You have little sense.

BETTY: No more messing around, Mary Magdalene. You and me settling it right here, right now. Clear the space… (*Aggressively to the DJ.*) and run the song!

KITTY: No showdowns until I perform!

A frantic folk song strikes up. BETTY and JUANA walk left and right like heated warriors to the tune. BETTY halts:

BETTY: Stop the music!

Music stops as she raps to JUANA.

I WATCHING YOU FOR YEARS, DOING DRAG ALL OVER TOWN.
DAYTIME AND NIGHT TIME, IN THAT TATTERED, DIRTY GOWN.
I THOUGHT YOU WERE A BAD THING, BUT NOW I SEE THE FRAUD.
YOU'S A FRIGHTENED, BEAT-UP JESUS FREAK. I'LL SEND YOU BACK TO GOD.

Run the song!

The music goes back to the frantic folk beat until JUANA shouts.

JUANA: Stop the music!

Silence.

I REMEMBER WHEN I WAS YOUNG. I REMEMBER WHEN I WAS FINE.
FROM THEN TO NOW I NEVER WORK LIKE ME ARSE WAS ON THE LINE.
WHEN I BEND MY KNEES TO PRAY, I THANK GOD I AIN'T THAT TART,
STEALING AND WHEELING, NEVER TO BE LEAVING THAT SHITTY PENNY MART.

Run the song!

The music starts again. They strut past each other in warrior frenzy.

BETTY: Hold the music!

THE WORK I DO IS LEGAL. I DON'T TAKE CASH FOR FREE.
BUT YOU'S A LONG TIME HO THAT HIDING BEHIND KITTY.
NOW ALL THAT NONSENSE DONE TONIGHT. I'M YIELDING TO
    TEMPTATION.
RIGHT HERE IN MY DIARY, SWEET THANG, IS THE NUMBER FOR
    IMMIGRATION!
RUN THE MUSIC AND PASS ME A PHONE. LET ME MAKE THAT
    CALL! TIME TO TAKE THE TRASH OUT!

The music starts.

JUANA: Stop the music. I said stop the music!!

ALL RIGHT, YOU TWO-LEFT FOOT BITCH — TREAT ME LIKE AN
    OUTSIDER.
I'M IN THIS COUNTRY LONGER THAN YOU IN BATTY-RIDER.
EVERYONE IN HERE KNOW ME. THEY KNOW THAT I IN THIS
    FIGHT.
BUT THAT MAN AIN'T SLAP YOU HARD ENOUGH. I WILL
    STRAIGHTEN YOUR TEETH TONIGHT!
PLAY IT LIKE YOU MEAN IT AND DON'T STOP TILL WE IN PRISON!

*BETTY lunges at JUANA. LUCY stops her. KITTY and
LUCY are caught in the middle.*

LUCY: Aye! Aye! Behave!!

KITTY: They won't stop. Handle them, Lucy. I'm going to
get my song in.

LUCY: No Kitty, it's me.

KITTY: *Miss* Kitty!

VASHTI: What the arse wrong with you, Lucy? You
convert?

LUCY: I never had a room sit up and listen to me before. I
want it.

KITTY: You'll go on after me and wrap up the show. Hold them if you want your chance. Come take over from me, Vashti.

VASHTI: And have one of them scratching hens give me salmonella? Forget it.

JUANA: Shut up and set me loose on that witch. I have the right to worship. She must learn that. Amen!

KITTY: Lucy, just do what butch men do with queens. Bash them.

LUCY: But…

KITTY exits.

BETTY: Let me get at her eyes.

LUCY: Listen to me! I squeeze into a bra tonight to try something different and I don't intend to waste my time! Anybody standing after I count to one and I will beat three of you so bad they will bury you in the same matchbox.

BETTY: S'cuse me? Who do you think…

LUCY: ONE!

LUCY makes to punch BETTY. They all scramble to their chairs. LUCY sits gently among them.

Look at my face now. All untidy. Someone pass me a brush.

JUANA: Here, Miss Lucy.

LUCY: Put the squabbles aside. We have little time left. You two are supposed to support Kitty. Think about that and help her. Vashti, think about me. Hold on for a little bit.

Lights out backstage. SUZY is downstage going down Memory Lane.

SUZY: (*Laughing.*) Oh yes, those were the days… Anyone here remember the jungle bunnies? One of you old reprobates must remember trekking through the forest to the hut hideout? That was my time. Honeys, when a handbag dropped down the lavatory we left it for the snakes. You think you wild now? One night I was singing to an eight track hooked up on a car battery. Bats were scattering round the hut, birds were screaming for help when suddenly: 'crack!' Everyone thought the villagers down the way found out and were coming with women and children to hack us to pieces. Juana jumped in the fridge, Mabel locked herself in the toilet and I dived through the window – dress and all. Sean was a year old and I could picture the scandal bout businessman being found. Meryl, you remember? You started saying the rosary. It was only Kitty. The drunken bitch climbed on the roof to sing, cut a hole with her heels and came crashing through. We laughed for weeks… (*Desperately.*) Come on Meryl, Barbara – somebody must remember. Anybody! For god's sake, that was my life! I was one of you then! …I really sacrificed a lot for Leandra, and she still keeps tracking me down to make sure I never get back into it. I'm just a relic now. I can't believe everybody forgot.

KITTY: (*From the wings.*) It's all right, Suzy. I remember.

SUZY: Thanks, Kitty. We both have scars from it. Mine is for my boy. Ladies and gentlemen. Let me bring on a lady who has weathered those days and more. This is the Grande Dame of the drag stage and my oldest friend. Boys and girls, before you forget us all – Miss Kitty Caress.

Song 8
Sung by KITTY with BETTY and JUANA

BETTY and JUANA do back up but the tension and rivalry between them grows until it escalates into violence.

JUANA and BETTY finally break into a fight. Everybody has to rush in to get them off the stage.

SUZY: Take them off the stage! Sorry about that, ladies and gentlemen. Just stay calm and remain in your seats. Don't move about, make noise or use your cell phones. Stop anyone you see making a call especially at the back. We have a problem tonight. Millie, if you'd said something before it wouldn't come to this!… I apologise unreservedly. We didn't expect anything like it. I think tonight was too ambitious by half.

Backstage brightens and SUZY remains lit forestage. JUANA and BETTY and are ready to go at it again.

BETTY: I want you out my face!

JUANA: What you going to do? I have it in for you for weeks now!

They rush for each other but KITTY grabs the fire bucket and throws sand over them.

BETTY / JUANA: (*Very loudly.*) Aaaah!!

KITTY: Whores – both of you! You have no respect for yourselves. Get out! Suzy, you were right. End the show now.

VASHTI: At last.

LUCY: What about me?

SUZY: I'll have to refund the tickets.

VASHTI: Does that mean we don't get paid?

KITTY: Get out before I call the police myself!

BETTY: Madam, you just put sand in my straight, glossy hair – grows like that from the roots, girls. You'd better pay me for a wash and cut.

JUANA: Beat that cheap rug with a stick!

BETTY: I'll beat you.

KITTY: Get out!

LUCY: Let me do my song first, Kitty. You don't even have to pay me.

KITTY: It's over, Lucy. I performed and I ain't hanging around to take licks for none of them. Barbara, Meryl and everybody had a good enough belly laugh. I wanted us to feel like real people for a change but they were right. Start the stampede, Suzy.

LUCY: No!

SUZY: Are you sure, Kitty?

KITTY: Let me hug a bottle of rum and forget the shame.

SUZY: Ladies and gentlemen, due to a technical emergency we have to ask you all to leave. Please do so in an orderly fashion. I wrote that line in case of a raid.

LUCY: No! Nobody move!

LUCY pulls a gun from his bra.

SUZY: What the…

BETTY: Bullets over, Miss Miller's! Girls duck!

LUCY: Tell them to stay, Suzy.

SUZY: Ladies and gentlemen, please stay.

JUANA: Don't shoot me. I need a priest first for last rites. You can gun me down after. I'll be okay.

VASHTI: What the hell you doing?

LUCY: You said dress up. I said no. You said do it for money. I said it ain't me. You said I get a chance to hide from the law and the posse. I agreed. I practised for weeks to be anybody but that boy that they want to beat, and for once in my life I will have it. I ain't going till somebody take a picture of me singing as Lucy!

VASHTI: Goodbye. Pa will finish me off if you don't.

LUCY fires a shot in the air. The others scream and crouch.

LUCY: I going down to prison and nothing can stop it. Mr Rampaul can't scare me with nothing I ain't been panicking about for months. Tonight is my night to prance and nobody going till I get it.

KITTY: You damn fool. That will echo for miles.

LUCY: Let them come. Anybody who want to argue, can argue with Percy – me gun.

SUZY: It's the same old shit, eh Kitty? What the hell? Let's go down in style. Sean ain't coming. Maybe with all the Carnival parties around nobody heard. (*Turning to the audience.*) Ladies and gentlemen, we had a faulty circuit blow up. But the show goes right on.

JUANA: (*To BETTY.*) Bitch, do you mind? You're stepping on my foot.

BETTY: I though you wanted to be like Jesus. Consider it a crucifixion.

JUANA: I will hit you again…

LUCY: Aye, behave yourselves. I am in charge now.

KITTY's mobile rings. She answers.

KITTY: It's my friend the Minister. He says…hold on… Two reports came already about a gunshot coming from the Sports Association. Wait…

JUANA: You're still on my pedicure!

BETTY: Christ should have been so lucky to get a Manolo Blahnik heel instead of a rusty nail.

JUANA: Blasphemy! Now I can die a martyr.

JUANA and BETTY begin fighting again.

KITTY: One report came from inside…and the voice was female. Suzy?

SUZY: You know what? I feel a song coming on.

KITTY: Suzy?

Song 1 – Reprise
Sung by ALL

SUZY: Go for drinkies, boys and girls. I'll get an electrician to sort out the circuit and be back, in say, fifteen… (*Shouts.*) MILLIE!!

Intermission.

ACT 2

*KITTY appears in the cabaret arena in traditional island costume.
BETTY and JUANA are also on but tied to chairs. LUCY stands
above, aiming her gun to make sure they perform.*

Medley
Sung by KITTY

KITTY: Now we're going to take you to downtown Port of
Spain in the old days where you can hear the market
vendor cry…

*KITTY turns to BETTY to be the market woman but BETTY
looks away in a huff. LUCY aims at KITTY. She has to sing
it herself.*

Now we go to an old time bar for a refreshing drink
from the island heat. Bar lady?!

*KITTY turns to JUANA but she also looks away. LUCY points
again and KITTY does it herself.*

*KITTY ends and BETTY and JUANA are dragged off. SUZY
enters.*

SUZY: Well, well, you're still here, loving our show
'Sparkle, Sparkle'. Most of you got the word about our
'difficulties', but I guess you feeling some Carnival
rebellion in your soul. I remember my Carnival history.
It was the British colonials trying to block people
dancing in the streets that made them rebel and create
Carnival. Nobody recorded a queen throwing a handbag
at the time. Wake up, boys and girls; grab your things
and go. You ever had a Trini policeman knee you to the
ground? (*To someone in the audience.*) You better not
answer that. It's not that kind of show… I'm only staying
because those girls thought I was getting depressed

73

under Leandra's regulations and tried to pull me out. You see, it was easy at first giving up my life for Sean when he was young, but as he got older and I got old, I felt old. It's the hot sun. Still, if you want to stay, feel free. I will see the girls through a little crisis back there. But you heard the big noise. You know what could happen if the neighbours heard. But you want carnival rebellion tonight. I'll give you Carnival rebellion. I have fifteen years of things I've been hoping to tell you boys and girls on a night like this. Get ready for my wish list starting with 'A' for arsehole lightman…

Backstage. BETTY and JUANA are bound to their chairs and gagged. LUCY admires her gun.

KITTY: What you going to do with that? You can't keep us here forever.

LUCY: 48 hours to Carnival and people already in the streets. Why stop the party?

KITTY: Don't be stupid. That damn shot probably blew Millie's cover. This party is dead from bullet wound. We have to clear out.

LUCY: I'm dressed up as Lucy, and you know what? I like her. That boy, Lucas, got this gun six months ago and he never had the guts to fire it. He run away from the damn shopkeeper… But Lucy didn't wait for a second. She made the whole place sit up… I don't want to shut this girl down yet.

VASHTI: Lucy, behave. You playing with things you don't understand, and I don't mean the gun. This bar going to be a battering zone and it's a battle running longer than you taking up a wig.

LUCY: What's the difference? We all living undercover, but I don't mind doing something about it. What you doing, *Miss* Kitty? You have your big shot friends; you know the Minister. Get him down here to stop the shit. Use your connections.

KITTY: It doesn't work like that. You know it.

LUCY: They does hide and send you to take the heat, and when the pressure on you run. You's a blasted coward! All of you! (*To VASHTI.*) You want to hide from your Pa when I knew you was a sissy from way back in school. This whole blasted Miss Miller set up is for cowards! Not Miss Lucy though. Only one lady and her gun to get everybody straight. We're doing the show. Who next?!

KITTY: Why don't you perform? That's what you want.

LUCY points the gun at KITTY.

LUCY: Then what? What you going to do while I'm out there?

KITTY: Little boy, you might frighten the others with your tool but it won't work on me. I've been through enough roughnecks to not care anymore.

LUCY: What you going to do, Kitty?

LUCY sticks the gun in KITTY's hip.

VASHTI: You're acting like a fool now.

KITTY: For God's sake just go on and leave us alone.

LUCY pushes the gun harder.

KITTY: (*Salaciously.*) Oooh…

VASHTI: I think she's enjoying it.

LUCY: You wouldn't enjoy it when I blow off your hip. What you going to do when I'm out there on my own?!

KITTY: (*Feeling threatened.*) Run out the back… What you expect? I didn't plan to truly get lynched tonight!

75

LUCY laughs raucously.

VASHTI: Stop acting like a crazy person.

LUCY: What you want of me again, Vashti; to go back and hide in the cowshed? I'm tired… I can't do it anymore. (*To KITTY.*) Get someone on. People waiting.

KITTY: Who?! One of these? They're not capable of anything. They're gutter rats.

KITTY takes the gag off JUANA.

JUANA: Let me at that bitch! I will crucify her upside down. She defiled me, Kitty, and…

KITTY puts the gag back on.

KITTY: (*To LUCY.*) They can't see further than a bra strap. They can only live for squeezing out what moment they get.

KITTY removes BETTY's gag.

BETTY: (*To KITTY.*) I will kill you!

KITTY: Me?

BETTY: I did everything for you: rehearsals, the lot. You should have recognised that I'm next in line to rule the scene but you chose that Spanish trash over me. I'm more than ghetto fabulous, girl. I should be queen over everything. But you messed up. I'm taking over. This is a coup!

VASHTI: You're tied to a chair, arsehole.

BETTY: A temporary setback, sugar, but you got to think positive. Call me your leader!

KITTY puts the gag back on.

KITTY: (*To LUCY.*) These girls have been put into a hole far deeper than you can pull them out of. Just let us go.

LUCY: Get someone on.

VASHTI: Lucy, listen to her.

LUCY: I don't want talk. The show continuing. Show some backbone!

KITTY: (*Sincerely.*) Honey, please. It's over. I'm a big enough fool for everybody. I don't need you to make it worse. When boys like you were playing cricket, I was working hard at dance and getting my leg up on a bar.

VASHTI: Times ain't changed much.

KITTY: Shut your face! My mother was a pioneer. But what was the point when nobody would allow a hen like me on stage anywhere unless it's to do a butch limbo? All I have is being camp and outrageous in every damn back hole because it's the only way I can still perform. It's the only way to forget I'm just a blasted dental nurse. But that won't change. Nobody wants me to be anything but dumb and camp so let's stop here and let it all go to hell!

VASHTI: Miss Kitty's right. We should think about going to the US so Ma and Pa can proudly lie about me to the village when I gone.

LUCY: What the arse is this? You walk the streets of Port of Spain like that at night but you panic when one man from the village turn up? I get shoved into a hole to be a bad boy and taking licks because me and me family ain't got money to be more than scum. Well, tonight I shoving back. Lucy ain't taking no more, and you all going to help or get your toes shot clean off.

KITTY: All right, sink us all. Take Betty out next if you must.

VASHTI: You going to untie that viper in here?

KITTY: No. She's a drag queen. Drag her out in the chair. She so damn greedy for raves she'll jump at the audience.

LUCY: (*Sarcastically.*) I'm glad you with me, Miss Kitty. Don't try nothing. I can see all sides. I'll shoot you in your tot tots.

LUCY drags BETTY out. KITTY buries her head in her hands.

KITTY: What we going to do?

VASHTI: I need to pee. Miss Kitty, you wouldn't mind helping unstrap me down there?

KITTY: Do I look like a lesbian? Go do it yourself!

VASHTI exits. KITTY paces nervously.

(*To JUANA.*) I wish you were of some help. How are we going to get out of here?

The lights dim and the spotlight comes on KITTY.

Suddenly, I feel off colour. Something tells me a pepper spray moment is coming on...

KITTY reaches into her handbag.

It's gone. Oh my god... SUZY!!!

Lights slam down backstage and brighten on SUZY forestage.

SUZY: 'S' – Space, coz in space no one can hear you scream. Well, this is space!...except when some of you scream outside coz the neighbours ready to hear it and act. And they're being led by a Pastor whom, when he says: 'you've got to pay for your sins', means in cash and blood. But when Mabel screamed no one heard, and when I scream in here, it's the proverbial tree falling in

the forest. That 'p' word too big for you? I keep
screaming that my ex-wife is draining my business as
revenge for breaking her heart but if I was six-foot-four
and still young, bitches like you, yes you that pass me
straight in the road, would want to listen. But when I
come here you still expect me to buy you drinks just to
get your company... Sometimes I wish I had it all...

Song 10
Sung by SUZY

And now 'T' – thongs. I don't understand why small
bottom women...

Lights slam to KITTY and a tied JUANA backstage.

KITTY: Promise you won't make noise when I take off the
gag. It's serious. We have to leave.

KITTY removes the gag.

JUANA: (*Very loud.*) Carajo, cuno de madre, CULO, voy a
matarla con mucho dolor, la puta, maricon...

KITTY slips the gag back on.

KITTY: Listen! All our weapons are gone – my pepper
spray, Vashti's Rambo knife... We've been caught.
Somebody's setting us up. You coming or not?

KITTY removes the gag.

JUANA: I am going to hack that Betty into little pieces –
one for each bead of the Rosary. She has no right telling
me, a Latin diva, that...

KITTY slips the gag back on.

KITTY: You stay and take it. I'm gone.

*KITTY tries to sneak out the door. LUCY's voice sounds
offstage.*

LUCY: One more step and a bullet will find your kneecaps.

KITTY: Oh God, help me.

Lights out and back to SUZY.

SUZY: 'X' – hmmm, that's a hard one. No. Ex-wife and you know about her. Look sweethearts, all I'm saying…

BETTY: Shut up and get off my blasted stage!

SUZY: Ladies and gentlemen, we seem to be back with loud mouth Betty.

Song 11
Sung by BETTY

BETTY exits. Lights out. KITTY and JUANA are still alone.

KITTY: Please, please – are you ready to be sensible?

KITTY removes the gag.

JUANA: I don't say this often, but my mouth is dry. … Mira guapa, Lucy's our only problem. If I try to leave I'll go to my maker with bullet holes in my soul – and I want Betty first.

KITTY: Juana, it's bigger than that. Whoever took our stuff is organised. It's been getting worse since Mabel got killed – like the whole nation got outraged to be reminded that we're still around.

JUANA: Honey, it's Vashti, Lucy and Rampaul playing games. Haven't you noticed Vashti's still here? Lucy wouldn't shoot her.

KITTY: (*In disbelief.*) No… yes?

VASHTI enters.

Sweetie, I'm seeing a bulge I shouldn't. Go back to the toilet.

VASHTI exits.

No…yes? No. Lucy can't see further than the excitement of lipstick. This is for real. I shouldn't have done the show and pulled everyone together to look like we're forming a resistance group.

JUANA: So what? Maybe we should. Maybe the spirit you felt is Mabel saying do it for her and yourself. After all Kitty, don't forget how we really met that Carnival…

KITTY: Shut up and don't be an ass! The police beat Mabel to death in front of onlookers and nobody reported a crime, nobody spoke up at the coroner's and nobody claimed her corpse. I don't want that. I only did the show to make a mark before we fade out. I mean we were the best. Look at Suzy, who would believe she was the most boisterous of all? But we mash up. That son of hers was a surprise enough but he should've been a good thing, not dragging her down to be a toothless bulldog. Vanity here is one thing, but the truth is I don't have it in me to face another hater. I've lost the guts for the worst – and you can't manage it either. Coming then?

JUANA nods to be untied. KITTY obliges.

JUANA: What about Suzy?

KITTY: We'll grab her off the stage. Everyone will follow. Lucy can't shoot us all.

They prepare to exit but have to back up as BETTY enters.

BETTY: Where do you think you're going? Why is she loose?

KITTY: All right, Juana, stay calm. Betty, my waters tell me the police know about us and they're going to strike any minute.

BETTY: And you two were going to run off and leave us like this. How nice. Makes the whole point of working five weeks together really worthwhile.

JUANA: When did you suddenly develop a heart? You've been a bitch the whole time.

BETTY: That's my nature, honey – bitch, bitch, bitch…! What about Miss Miller and everyone that came to see us? You're going to leave them too? Sometimes, I swear those musty women at the make-up counter are better people than you two.

JUANA: Stay here and take it then. You can dance for the forces.

BETTY: Why not? They loved me out there again. At least, I feel like a beauty queen instead of a fool around you two.

JUANA: Betty, chica, they're going to beat your face to a pulp. As much as it would help, I'd like to know you were safe so I can do it later.

BETTY: My face? Why didn't you say that before? Let's go. What about Lucy?

KITTY: It's either we disarm her, face the police division or get out now. Let's huddle together.

JUANA: You go first, Betty.

BETTY: (*Sarcastically.*) Thanks for nothing.

They begin to exit but have to back up as VASHTI enters.

KITTY: Oh Jesus, what next?

VASHTI: Where you all going?

BETTY: It's like this. We noticed that…

JUANA: Don't tell her, you fool. She's Lucy's friend.

BETTY: Look honey, we have loyalty in this country. She might want to come.

JUANA: Maybe she's in on it. Why hasn't Rampaul done anything yet? Maybe, Rampaul, Lucy and her leaked us to the police to save Lucy going to jail. Maybe they're in some kind of love triangle.

VASHTI: What?

JUANA: Come clean, Vashti. Why are you still here?

KITTY: (*Sarcastically.*) Why don't we all chat about it for another hour?

JUANA: Try to think a little further than lipstick, Betty. You'll get the whole picture.

BETTY: Look babe, don't tell me what to do. That is the biggest load of rubbish I ever heard. Reading too much Old Testament is warping your brain.

JUANA: Now, you see that's why you and I have a problem; that's why we can't get along. You don't seem to be able to respect I have a spiritual side instead of always lifting my skirt for a laugh.

BETTY: Honey, you're ashamed to be a drag queen. Why don't you just say it?

JUANA: There's no talking to you. Round two – right here, right now!

KITTY: For God's sake, we're on the run. Don't have a Jesus fit now.

LUCY enters.

(*To JUANA.*) See what you caused? It's a simple movement from here to the backdoor. What do I have to do, dangle a crucifix for you to follow?

JUANA: What do you mean by that?

LUCY: What going on?

KITTY: Out of my way. I want to leave.

JUANA: What do you mean by that, Kitty?

KITTY: Get your blasted act together! I'm fed up of worrying what you will do if somebody mentions church and Juana in the same sentence. Clear your conscience. Nobody asked you to do drag. I want to go!

BETTY: She come here to hide among us because she didn't have the guts to do it in she own country.

JUANA: (*To KITTY.*) How long do I have to put up with everyone treating me like I don't belong?

KITTY: Who cares about that? Who cares about anything you do? So, you live with an old man and you want to beat yourself up about it. Who gives a shit? I'm stuck here because of you.

JUANA: What do you want to know, Kitty? How I fit prayer and lipstick in my head? In my country, I grew up with duty – a duty to everything that is right and sacred. I left because I hated that duty. I spat at it – there like that. (*He spits on BETTY.*) But I haven't forgotten what is right and sacred, and what is right and sacred is that after all this, I go to my priest and confess that I strap down my crotch, slip into stockings and paint my nails and love it. I am a drag queen, my dear, and I will be to the day I die. But I was born a Catholic. I still have a duty to confess my sins. Move aside, Lucy. I'm going on stage to do what I came to this country for.

KITTY: Juana, you can't.

JUANA: Run if you want to. I also have a duty to the people who stayed.

JUANA exits.

LUCY: I only asked what going on?

Lights out backstage and brighten on SUZY forestage.

SUZY: And I'm telling you, as in the words of a famous calypso, that I never eat a white meat yet. And I'm getting a serious case of the munchies so the tourists in the house looking good. It's not a gun in my pocket it's a bottle of ketchup. I will get the carving set out later but first I want to thank you for coming. I don't think the show will go on much longer but it's a record we had one at all. I want to big up Millie for sticking her neck out and giving us a regular place to hide. And a big, big up to my ladies for fighting through hell and high water – and I mean that literally – to sing for you and Mabel. I'll return to obscurity with my DVDs, dog and cat, but at least I felt a spark of old times…/

JUANA: Ay Suzy, I'm ready.

SUZY: Feel the love. Juana La Venezolana.

Song 12
Sung by JUANA

SUZY: I told you we were international. You can't call me a liar. But you can call me anytime, and anywhere. As the clock ticks down to potential disaster, and Millie is hurriedly bagging the takings to make a safety dash to Barbados, I just want to say that I'm feeling like family here for a change. This is cheaper than therapy. I should've chatted with you instead of shelling out on electric shock treatment. The shrink though was well…

Lights go out on SUZY. JUANA enters the dressing room in a troubled mood.

LUCY: (*To KITTY.*) Who next? (*To JUANA.*) What happen to you?

JUANA: Out there... I saw Rampaul waving. He wanted us to clear out – not us – you, Vashti. What going on between you and that man?

VASHTI: Nothing. If he says go, that's good enough for me.

JUANA: I don't like it, Kitty.

LUCY: Who care about that? I feel real bad now. Nobody could do us anything. We will show them they can't trample small people. We will tell our grandchildren about the night of revolution.

BETTY: Grandchildren? Now, I know she's lost it.

LUCY: Hush your mouth! We not backing down. We will see it to the end.

KITTY: I agree with Lucy.

JUANA: Eh?

KITTY: She's right. How long are we going to take this nonsense? We decided to do a show and we're that close to finish. To run now is to take shame. Let's stand up for once. Lucy, you next.

LUCY: Don't try that one, Kitty. I ain't born yesterday.

KITTY: Vashti won't go and we've done our songs.

JUANA: Kitty's right. My Latin fire is ignited now. We'll go down in a blaze of glory.

LUCY: You all lying, right?

BETTY: Why should they lie? We still have people left, and as long as there's an audience, everyone must perform to prove I'm the best. Do it, sweetheart.

LUCY: ... Thank you, girls! I'm going to get all teary. You don't know what it means to me to be with you for the past weeks and...

KITTY: Save it, love. You need freshening. We can't let you on like that. Girls, help me. I think you know what we need to do.

KITTY crowds in on LUCY and powders his face in a dizzying fluster.

JUANA: Yes, cariña. Those shoes need tightening. Lift your foot.

BETTY: Let me fix that wig, girl. It's not decent.

The three are all over LUCY.

KITTY: Girls on three. One, two, three!

BETTY pulls the wig over LUCY's eyes. JUANA lifts LUCY's leg higher and KITTY shoves him over as BETTY pulls the gun from his hand.

Damn fool. I still have standards in a crisis. You think I'd ever let you on? Suzy! (*Showing the gun.*) We got it. Keep it going till we come get you.

Lights brighten on SUZY downstage as KITTY shows him the gun.

SUZY: Ladies and gentlemen, our problem backstage is solved but the one out here isn't, so you can leave now if you like – or wait a little. It seems I still have to hold on.

Backstage.

BETTY: Let's go. This face has to be saved for future users.

VASHTI: Come on, Lucas; give me your hand.

LUCY: Don't call me that! I'm Lucy!

VASHTI: The show is over, you understand?! It's over!

LUCY: Don't leave me, Vashti. You're the only person who ever looked out for me.

VASHTI: What you want me to do, risk losing my family? I already waited all night for you. I can't do anymore. I'm leaving the cowshed unlocked. You choose.

KITTY takes a last look around.

KITTY: It was worth trying, wasn't it?

JUANA: It was, chica. Let's go.

They begin to exit but LEANDRA forces them to re-enter.

LEANDRA: Hold on! Too late! Back it up, batty boys! Back up! And give me that. (*She takes the gun from KITTY.*)

BETTY: Who is this bitch?

LEANDRA: So, this is where you perform your gender transformation. Sick.

VASHTI: Is she real?

LEANDRA: I was born with my body parts, if that's what you mean. Sit down, all of you. You're not going anywhere. Your pervert games are over.

LEANDRA surveys the room with scorn, and then KITTY.

Keith, is that you?

VASHTI: You know her?

LEANDRA: What would your mother say if she saw you like this? You have no shame? I told you to stop this nastiness but you wouldn't listen. I told you to keep it away from my family. You're about to learn the hard way.

JUANA: Somebody take her batteries out, please. We have to go.

LEANDRA: Go where? You're such fools. Look into the light. I want to introduce you to Police Officer Phillip of the Vice Squad who is also the Pastor of The Reformed Reunited Union of The Episcopal Evangelical Baptist Church round here. He's my friend and accomplice. He couldn't believe this was going in his parish until I convinced him. And you (*LUCY*), holding up the raid with this stupid gun. I was hoping you would shoot them. You're the man here. But you let them corrupt you. You made me suffer through the whole show.

BETTY: Woman, I don't know who you are, but I'll knock out you and Officer Pastor Phillip if you knock my performance.

LEANDRA: Shut up. I know you. You're the hen in the Penny Mart and I know the people you work for. You won't know me, of course, 'cause I don't shop there. But I can officially tell you you're fired! That's what real women do. What's wrong with all of you? You have no respect for yourselves or anybody?

SUZY enters.

SUZY: Leandra. I should've known. Sorry ladies, her collar must have come loose.

LEANDRA: (*Deeply affected.*) Harold, my God…look at you. Why? You promised…

SUZY: Fifteen years ago, Leandra. It's a long time.

LEANDRA: It doesn't expire. What if someone we know were to see you dressed as a woman? How could you go back to this?

SUZY: Where's Sean?

LEANDRA: At home. You expected him to come to this den? He doesn't need a father to be ashamed of.

SUZY: Or a mother to think for him.

LEANDRA: He's not on your side. He sold you out. That's how I know about tonight. He left it to me to take care of things as usual, and I've done better than that.

KITTY: The lightman is a police officer.

SUZY: That explains why he has no taste.

LEANDRA: Let me look at you close up, look at the other woman. How stupid to think you were having an affair because I found a bra and lipstick in the glove compartment. It was an affair with yourself.

SUZY: Leave me alone. You have Sean.

LEANDRA: Correction, Harold. You have the business. If the nation finds out about you, Sean will have nothing. That's why I called the police in.

SUZY: Tell him to switch off.

LEANDRA: That depends on you. I made an arrangement with the Officer Pastor there. He doesn't want this scandal in his backyard. You can all walk free. Millie will have a few months to move – providing you make heavy donations to his church. That is after you take off that nastiness once and for all and hand over the business to Sean.

SUZY: You asked him if he wants it?

LEANDRA: I make the decisions! Listen to me, if you don't comply the police will come in and smash this whole damn place, them and Millie to pieces. (*To KITTY.*) Don't try contacting your Minister friend because he's the one that has them lined up outside waiting on my word. Yes, following you led us to his dirty lifestyle. He ain't having any party for you. I don't think he made any preparations.

BETTY: (*To SUZY.*) You were married to that? I hope you have your divorce papers framed in gold.

LEANDRA: Shut your batty mouth! I'm sorry I didn't let the dog loose on your tail earlier.

JUANA: (*To BETTY.*) See?

KITTY: But Leandra…

LEANDRA: How dare you call my name? Take that damn wig off and look at yourself. You're a man!

She rips KITTY's wig off and goes for JUANA.

And you – letting children see you like that in the daytime – you should be torched.

She rips JUANA's wig off as well and grabs LUCY's.

You bring decent people down! You're bringing my son down! You're depraved! Twisted!… (*She goes for BETTY's wig.*)

BETTY: Don't think about it, girl.

She skips BETTY.

LEANDRA: They should kill your arse!

She grabs VASHTI's hair.

VASHTI: Ouch!

LEANDRA: (*Surprised.*) It's real? All of it?

VASHTI: Yes.

LEANDRA: My god, it's so lustrous. How do you get that shine? I try with mine but I can never get it to hold…What am I saying? You're corrupting me.

SUZY: Satisfied now? If it's me you're after then go for me.

91

LEANDRA: (*Laughing.*) Now, you're talking like a man. You feel a silly woman like me can only be hooked on that thing between your legs that you don't want.

SUZY gets angry and shakes her.

SUZY: Let me breathe! You have my whole damn life stitched up. You didn't have to endanger everybody. But you're still vex with me. Say it!

LEANDRA: Yes! I keep jumping from boyfriend to boyfriend. But every time I start over I have to hide the truth about you because I can't even explain it to myself. Why'd you do it? I gave up everything to be with you. I was happy having a home and a son. But you lied to me. We used to meet and chat as friends but you pushed it further – and I believed you. Do you remember what you said to me all those years ago?

Song 13
Sung by LEANDRA and SUZY

You stripped me of everything, Harold, Suzy or whatever you call yourself. Now, I want you to strip right down and burn that nastiness out of you. I brought kerosene and matches. Take everything off, put it there and promise you will never do it again.

VASHTI: Horror flash. That's like me in the village when Mr Rampaul caught me.

LUCY: But it never stopped you. You came right back out and did it again. What the hell really going on here?

LEANDRA: Stop the batty talk. Strip, Harold – or I'll let the police break in. I want closure.

LUCY: What you doing, Vashti? What all of you doing? Vashti, I meet you, more than once, walking the streets of Port of Spain, and more than once boys pelt you with bottle and threaten to kill you. And what you do? Tell them to go home and send their fathers, flashing Rambo like a warrior. You going to run from she and Rampaul to the US? Why you don't tell then the truth about you and Rampaul?

VASHTI: I don't want to talk about it.

JUANA: Lucy's right. I ran from my country so no one would pull my wig off and bundle me to church for penance. Look at me. When does it stop?

BETTY: My hair's still on right.

JUANA: Because you're a dumb bitch. What did you do when that man slapped you?

LEANDRA: Shut up. You're dangling on a knife-edge.

BETTY: I ran. These are expensive imported nails. I wasn't going to break one hitting back.

JUANA: We never hit back, sugar. That's what we're good at.

BETTY: Because none of you was going to support me! You weren't going to find him and say 'don't do that here'. Kitty won't even acknowledge my talent. I'm on my own. Every day in that Penny Mart I dream of being a beauty queen 'cause that keeps me going. But if I say it here you knock me. That's why I'm a bitch. We're not a team.

JUANA: And Kitty's not Kitty anymore. Just a dental nurse. Hi, Keith.

KITTY: Leave it alone, Juana. Leandra, I'm sorry. The show was my idea. Negotiate with the police, please. I shouldn't have done it.

LEANDRA: I don't care about you. You were the problem then and you're the problem now. I wish they kill you. We'd be better off.

KITTY: What?

JUANA: Dead, chica, as in non-existent, as in never walking the planet…

KITTY: I heard her!

JUANA: Shall I tell them how we really met or will you?

KITTY: Be quiet!

JUANA: Kitty wasn't drunk in a drain that Carnival Tuesday…

KITTY: No, I wasn't drunk! I was a posh bitch from the better side of town. We occasionally did the jungle bunnies, didn't we Suzy? But usually we'd be in a fancy house where somebody's wife was out the country. We had one in yours, Leandra.

LEANDRA: Lord, now I'm ready to murder. Harold start or I'll give the signal.

SUZY: All right!

KITTY: Don't you dare! The truth is I didn't like hiding. I was like Betty, an attention seeker.

BETTY: Your memory stretches that far back?

KITTY: I went into town that Carnival Tuesday to get a whole street audience. Who would've cared about a boy in a dress? I wanted to woo them. With enough rum in their veins they were going to love me, make me Carnival queen, show me love and freedom in the midday sun. What they did was beat the shit out of me because I was sailing too close to real. They wanted me dead. People like you Leandra, wanted me dead. And here we are, so many Carnivals later, and you still want him, them and me dead? Fuck you! You fucked up my wig and I don't like it. I should've crawled out the drain but I waited for her and her angels to find me. Tonight I

will do it myself. Juana, can you acquire me my hair
installation?

JUANA: Today feels like a good day to die. Bendigame,
Kitty.

KITTY: And how dare you talk about my mother?! She
paid for ballet lessons. She would've been here to
strangle a policeman herself but she's ill. It's time I stop
playing the ass and make her proud. Suzy, I'm ready to
entertain the boys in blue. Joining?

VASHTI: Wait… Everybody seems to be getting high-
minded and I want to go home. Suzy's lived like this for
a long time. What's another forty years or so? Miss
Leandra must die some time. She's offering us a way out.
Let's take it.

LUCY: And go where – to the US? This is our country. I
ain't going. Let them deal. If I survive tonight I will
become a librarian. That's what I want but nobody ever
see it and I was too ashamed to say. But if you all could
dress like that then it still have room on this island for
me to live a dream. I ain't running. Why you don't tell
them 'bout you and Rampaul? Tell them!

VASHTI: He's in love with me. I take intimidation and
threats every day to give in. He's a desperate old
man…but I'm really in love with Lucas.

LUCY: Well, Lucas don't need a coward. (*LUCY begins to
shove VASHTI.*) Run from me, run from your Pa, from
she…

LEANDRA: Stop or I'll shoot.

LUCY: Go on – run!!

VASHTI: (*Shoving back hard.*) Don't push me!

LUCY: That's the Vashti I know. You don't take shit. Them police didn't come this far to go back empty-handed. When you going to stop running? Let's make a stand.

JUANA: Join us, mija. It's either that, or go down in shame.

VASHTI: I hope Pa have bail money. I hope one of you will mind me.

KITTY: Suzy?

LEANDRA: It's Harold. Take your blows on your own. Don't pull him back in.

SUZY: Kitty, I can't.

LEANDRA: It's Keith!

KITTY: Sean will never come.

LEANDRA: You're damn right. I don't know what he was thinking. Imagine he was fighting me to come here. As if I'd ever let him out the house to see you.

SUZY: You mean he was coming?

LEANDRA: Don't get any stupid ideas. Get out of those clothes and burn them for all times. Let me see it. I hope you brought something decent to go home in. Could you imagine the press taking a photograph of father and son in the same illegal dive? I have to think of everything.

SUZY: (*Joyously.*) So, he was coming. Oh Leandra, you want me to strip down? Fine.

SUZY strips to corset, stockings, garters and high heels.

LEANDRA: Oh my God! You wear that underneath? You need help.

BETTY: Nice set. Where'd you buy that?

SUZY: Forget it, bitch. You couldn't afford this on a year of Penny Mart salary.

KITTY: The bitch is back. Missed you, honey. Just landed?

SUZY: I've been to paradise, girl – but I've never been to me.

JUANA: I hear that's a shit hole in the public toilets. I wouldn't go to you either.

SUZY: You remember the line, Spanish whore.

LEANDRA: Are you mad?

SUZY: This is the real me, Leandra. It's sick or whatever you want to call it. I screwed up your life and I'm sorry. But I've just found Sean and I don't want to be a liar to him – not anymore. Girls, we have a finale to do!

LEANDRA: Take that off, Harold or I'll make the call. I'm in control. I'm serious. None of you will get hurt if he undresses.

There's a sudden heavy pounding against a door at the back offstage.

(*Scared.*) What's that?

JUANA: The police are here. Let's strike up the chorus, girls.

LEANDRA: That's impossible. They're waiting for my word.

JUANA: That's more than the police. It's the whole neighbourhood.

SUZY: I guess your Pastor didn't want batty money. He can make more of a name by cleaning up the perverts. He set you up too.

LEANDRA: No, Harold, he wouldn't do that. I have it organised. I'm still in here.

SUZY: This is hate, Leandra. You know what hate is? I've been living with it all my life, and we're always the ones to get it. Tell Sean I went down with a fight. Young people like that. It's like PlayStation. Tell him I was Lara Croft, but bigger at the top.

The sound of police sirens are heard.

LEANDRA: Oh God, they tricked me. Come with me, Harold.

JUANA looks out over the audience.

JUANA: Millie's holding on to Periwinkle to attack. Someone talk to Millie. She thinks she's Calamity Jane. She is though, isn't she?

SUZY: It's been a long time coming for this bar.

LEANDRA: Harold, come! I don't want you dead.

KITTY looks out.

KITTY: These people are still sitting down out there. They must really love us or they want to get embroiled in the mess. Barbara and Meryl are reaching in their handbags for weapons… I don't want to mention what they just pulled out. All right, girls – get into costume. First time drag show, girls – and first time show down. We have a number to perform.

The girls begin getting dressed.

LEANDRA: Please Harold, I can protect you.

SUZY: From what? This is the one space we have, and they want to take it. Just tell Sean. Promise me… Promise!

LEANDRA: All right.

SUZY: Now sit down bitch, and stay out of my way… Stay out of harm's way, love. I don't want them to hurt you.

LUCY: You all right, Vashti?

VASHTI: I just shit right through my sari. I am going to the USA though. That hasn't changed.

LUCY: We'll be okay.

KITTY: Are we ready, girls?

JUANA: Si.

LUCY: Suzy, you don't know the finale.

SUZY: Honey, I've watched that old bitch rehearse it so many times I can do it backwards.

BETTY: If we get out of this alive we must meet up and be friends. I like your style.

SUZY: Someone kill me now!

There's a huge crunching of wood as if the police just made their way through.

KITTY: Millie, give us our song, and try to sing on key, ladies. Please make me proud. Now, glitter in your minds. They can't get you there.

SUZY: It's really Carnival here tonight.

SUZY steps forward from the dressing room to forestage.

Ladies and gentlemen, we've made it to the end of the evening and we're moist that you stayed on. I speak for the girls and myself when I say that you're the best and only audience we've ever had and we would have you any time as long as you put some cash down first. It's time for our finale. Here, for the last time, I give you the scintillating… I love that word…the scintillating… well… Boys and girls, let's say au revoir and not farewell as I demand on stage the daring, the fabulous Carnival Barbies!

The others join SUZY and form a fighting troupe.

Medley 2
Sung by ALL

LUCY steps forward and sings in the medley.

They take their bows as the shouts of policemen's voices are heard in the back. They continue.

Fade to black.

End.

List of songs